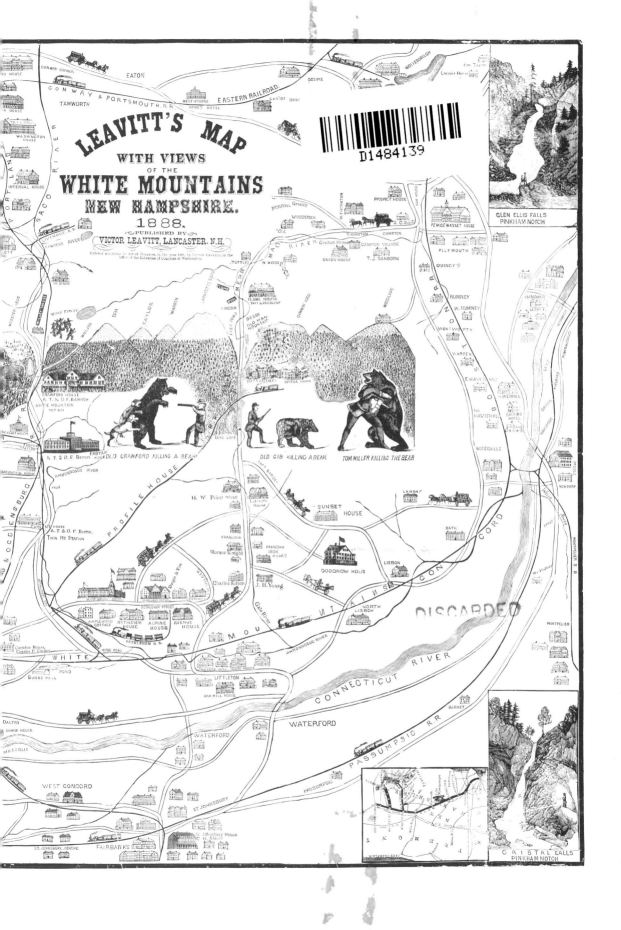

LEAVITT'S MAP

WITH VIEWS
OF THE
WHITE MOUNTAINS
NEW HAMPSHIRE.
1888.

PUBLISHED BY
VICTOR LEAVITT, LANCASTER, N.H.

Entered according to Act of Congress, in the year 1887, by Victor Leavitt, in the office of the Librarian of Congress at Washington.

OLD CRAWFORD KILLING A BEAR

OLD GIB KILLING A BEAR

TOM MILLER KILLING THE BEAR

GLEN ELLIS FALLS PINKHAM NOTCH

CRISTAL FALLS PINKHAM NOTCH

DISCARDED

Yesterday's

New Hampshire

Seemann's Historic States Series No. 2

Yesterday's

NEW HAMPSHIRE

By Richard F. Leavitt

WITH A FOREWORD BY SHERMAN ADAMS

E. A. Seemann Publishing, Inc.
Miami, Florida

974.2
L

Library of Congress Cataloging in Publication Data

Leavitt, Richard Freeman.
  Yesterday's New Hampshire.

  (Seemann's historic states series, no. 2)
  1. New Hampshire--Description and travel--Views.
2. New Hampshire--History--Pictorial works. I. Title.
F35.L42   917.42'03'0222   74-75295
ISBN 0-912458-39-9

974.2

To Fran Hughes, and the memory of Charlie
for a thousand yesterdays

CAPT. JOHN SMITH'S remarkably accurate map of New England. (PPL)

Preface

MY AIM in this book was to assemble from photographs taken throughout the years, some of the people, the places, and the events which have influenced, or in some way left their mark, upon the face and character of the Granite State. While the selection is a personal one, I have tried to include pictures which, hopefully, catch some of the special flavor that was yesterday in New Hampshire.

I am indebted to a score of people throughout the state who were unfailingly helpful. Library personnel include Mrs. Catherine Morrow of the New Hampshire Historical Society; Dorothy Vaughn and Sherman Pridham at the Portsmouth Public Library; Robert McDermand at the Herman H. Lamson Library in Plymouth; Kenneth Cramer and Wendy Tulgham at the Baker Memorial Library in Hanover; Stephen Powell, from special collections at UNH in Durham; Kay Fox at the Keene Public Library; Bob Lauze at the New Hampshire Archives, and Ann Doak at DRED in the State House Annex.

I would also like to express my appreciation to Dick Hamilton, Mary Nugent, Harry Alls, Douglas Philbrick, Murray Clark, Carroll Reed, Denton Hartley, Bill McClintock, and especially Peter Randall, editor of "*New Hampshire Profiles*" magazine, and former Governor Sherman Adams for his foreword.

I owe thanks to Houghton Mifflin Company of Boston for permission to quote from *New Hampshire—A Guide to the Granite State* (American Guide Series) copyright 1938; to the George H. Browne-Robert Frost collection, Herbert H. Lamson Library, Plymouth, N.H., copyright 1943, for permission to reprint the photo of Robert Frost.

7

The list of professional photographers whose work through the years has illuminated the face of New Hampshire is a long one, but several names would appear on every man's list. They include: Winston Pote (the dean of New Hampshire photographers), Guy Shorey, Harold Orne, Stephen Whitney, Dick Smith, and Douglas Armsden.

Lastly, I would like to thank Robert Shaw for his unfailing help at all times.

The Colebrook House   RICHARD F. LEAVITT
Colebrook, N.H.

FORMER GOVERNOR Sherman Adams with a fox trap. (AP)

8

Foreword

WHOEVER OBSERVED that music provided the one universal language did not foresee the developments that have been made in the techniques of modern photography. Pictures do provide the medium of communication that brings to life the history and culture of a State or Nation and provides a greater sense of the "feel" of the events the author tries to describe in the written word. Pictures can provide a visual "interpretation" of what he writes, and the means of understanding what life was like in the era he attempts to recapture.

Such is the design of *Yesterday's New Hampshire.* While many of the faces have changed or disappeared, the back-drops of the scenes of forests, lakes, and mountains are not different from those of centuries ago, or will be in the years ahead. To have collected, reproduced, and preserved these pictures is a contribution to the recorded history of that era and an indication of a growing awareness that much of our history has been, and still continues to be, lost through the absence of incentive to accomplish the task this author has set for himself.

It is reassuring to take note of the efforts of those who are beginning to pick up the remaining dangling threads of history and, through research, oral history, photography and film, to preserve the remnants of that history.

Since the days of Jeremy Belknap, historians have left great gaps in the written, pictorial, and audible history of New Hampshire. The recognition of this has prompted the work this author has undertaken, and the results are portrayed in these pages for those who have an affection for this State.

If these pages create for the reader a living image of earlier days and give him something to understand and remember of the events that are here brought back to life, it will have accomplished its purpose.

SHERMAN ADAMS

March 24, 1974

PASSACONAWAY (Son of the Bear) was the first
ruler of New Hampshire. A staunch advocate for peace,
he concluded alliances with over a dozen tribes in northern New England, and kept them from sweeping the settlers into the sea. Tradition holds that he was a great
magician; that he made water burn, swam the Merrimack in one breath, and created a living snake from the
skin of a dead one. Upon his death, he wrapped himself
in his symbolic robe of bearskin, said farewell to his subjects and mounted a sled drawn by twenty-four wolves
of mammoth size. He lashed them, screaming with religious joy, up and down hills, through valleys, and finally,
up Mount Washington where he gained the summit with
unslacked speed, and rode into the clouds where he was
forever lost to view. (NHP)

Yesterday's New Hampshire

THE FIRST VOYAGER to New Hampshire shores of whom there is any record was Captain Martin Pring, who, in June, 1603, sailed ten or twelve miles up the Piscataqua River and saw "goodly groves and woods and sundry sorts of beasts, but no people."

Two years later the coast of New Hampshire was visited by Samuel de Champlain, French explorer, who entered Piscataqua Bay on July 15, 1605, and probably landed at what is now known as Odiorne's Point, in the town of Rye.

The following year (1606), King James I of England issued a patent generally cited as the first Virginia Charter. In it the King claimed the right to colonize American lands from Cape Fear River, North Carolina, to Halifax, Nova Scotia. The territory was divided into two parts, and called North and South Virginia. While the South Virginia Company succeeded immediately in establishing at Jamestown the first permanent English colony in the New World, the North Virginia, or Plymouth Company completely failed to secure even a foothold in its part of the grant, including the section now known as New Hampshire, until the Pilgrims first landed at Provincetown before settling at Plymouth in 1620.

In 1614, Captain John Smith, whose many exploits have given him a permanent place in American history, ranged the shore from the Penobscot River in Maine to Cape Cod in Massachusetts, and during this voyage discovered the Isles of Shoals, giving them the name of Smith's Isles, and also the Piscataqua River which he found to be "a safe harbor with a rocky shore." Returning to England, he published there a description of the country, with a map of the seacoast. He presented the publication to Prince Charles, who gave the country the name of "New England."

Chiefly through the determined and persistent efforts of Sir Ferdinando Gorges, Governor of Plymouth, England, Captain John Smith, Captain John Mason, a London merchant, and a few others, a new charter was obtained in 1620 for the Plymouth Company, re-incorporated as the Council of New England, for a grant between the 40th and 48th latitudes, "from the Atlantic Ocean to the South Sea." Within these limits the Council was authorized to establish and govern settlements and to lease, sell, and otherwise dispose of its territory and its privileges, either to individuals or to proper interests. Among the recipients of the larger grants were Captain John Mason and Sir Ferdinando Gorges, who in 1622 received a joint patent to all land between the Merrimack and Kennebec Rivers, then called the Province of Maine.

Among those who received smaller grants from the Plymouth Council were David Thomson, who landed with a handful of colonists at Odiorne's Point near Portsmouth in 1623, and Edward Hilton, to whom a grant was given in 1631 of Hilton's Point, now Dover. This latter grant set forth that Hilton and his associates had at their own expense transported servants, built houses, and planted corn at Hilton's Point, and intended to develop the country. Whether the first settlement in New Hampshire was at Portsmouth or Dover is still a moot question, although general historical judgment favors Portsmouth.

In 1629, Mason and Gorges apparently came to an agreement regarding the division of the grant of the Province of Maine by which Mason secured a separate grant from the Council of Plymouth to that part of the territory which lay to the southeast of the Piscataqua River. In honor of the English county of Hampshire, where he had lived, he called it New Hampshire.

With a view to getting a share of the rich fur trade of Canada, Mason, Gorges and others obtained in 1629 a rather indefinite grant of land known as the Laconia Grant, west of the Merrimack and Kennebec Rivers, bordering on Lake Champlain and extending thence westward to Lake Ontario and north to the St. Lawrence. Over this territory, which was considered simply as a region for commercial exploitation, the only government was the immediate direction of agents appointed by the proprietors. These agents were treated as a body of workmen and controlled in a manner similar to that in which the Hudson Bay Company controls its factors. New Hampshire's first town government was established by popular vote in Dover in 1633, and its first church was organized there in the same year.

At that time there were few women in this region, for Ambrose Gibbons, one of the early settlers, wrote to his employer, Captain Mason, in 1634, that "maids, they are soone gonne in this countrie." Men worked for "four and six pounds" a year, and seldom received that. Food and clothes were scarce. Gibbons said that for himself, wife, child, and four men he had but half a barrel of corn and only one piece of meat for three months. Industry, however, was slowly developing. As early as 1631, sawmills and gristmills were built near Portsmouth, and iron ore was shipped to England three years later.

It was Captain Mason's intention to establish a semi-feudal domain in the New World, and under his direction actual settlement began. After his death in 1635, since he had never received a penny for all his outlay in the plantations, his widow virtually told the colonists to shift for themselves. His heirs, however, received their claims for lands that were being colonized in a welter of grants with confusing and overlapping boundaries. Litigation, known as the Masonian Controversy, continued until 1787.

The settlements at Portsmouth and Dover were followed by those at Exeter (1638) and Hampton (1639). These four towns became in reality four independent republics. Since they felt they were too weak to stand alone, the four towns in 1641 put themselves under the jurisdiction of Massachusetts, since it was expressly granted that "each town send a deputy to the General Court though they be not at present church members." All local affairs pertaining to law, learning, and religion were debated and decided by the voters of the town in purely democratic assemblies. Officers were elected at town meetings and, as the King's commissioners of revenue later reported, "the lowest mechanics discussed the most important points of government with the utmost freedom." By order of the Massachusetts General Court, corn and beans were to be used in voting for councilors, the corn indicating a favorable vote, the beans the contrary. The population of New Hampshire at this time was about 1000.

A year after the union with Massachusetts, the first New England law on Education was passed. It required masters and parents to provide instruction for their children, and was followed by the Act of 1647 which required the towns to furnish public education. Higher education too, was valued, for in 1600 Portsmouth voted to contribute sixty pounds a year toward the support of Harvard College.

Little colonization was done outside of the four original towns. For nearly a century Portsmouth was the seat of government and the center of influence. Some further exploration of the state was carried on, however, in 1642, by Darby Field, Captain Neal, and Henry Jocelyn, who discovered the White Mountains, Field being the first white man to scale Mount Washington.

The settlers in New Hampshire, unlike those of Massachusetts Bay Colony, came here mainly for commercial rather than religious reasons. Although Hampton, Dover, and Exeter were Puritan, Portsmouth made the Anglican its established church. In all the settlements, however, there was little persecution of those who differed in religious matters.

Exceptions that proved the rule of toleration then existing in New Hampshire were the hanging of two Quakers, William Robinson and Marmaduke Stevenson on October 27, 1659, for "returning to the province after banish-

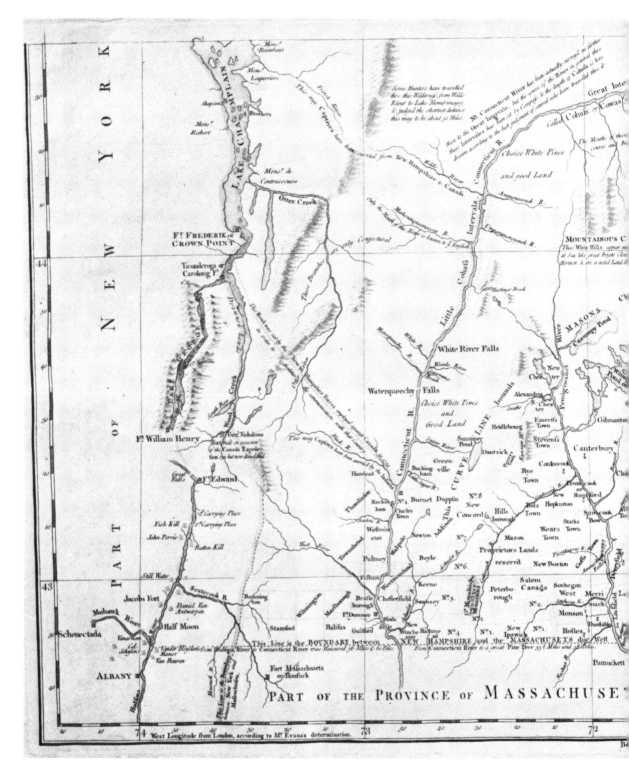

MAP OF MASON'S CLAIM — the longest and most confusing litigation in the history of New Hamp-

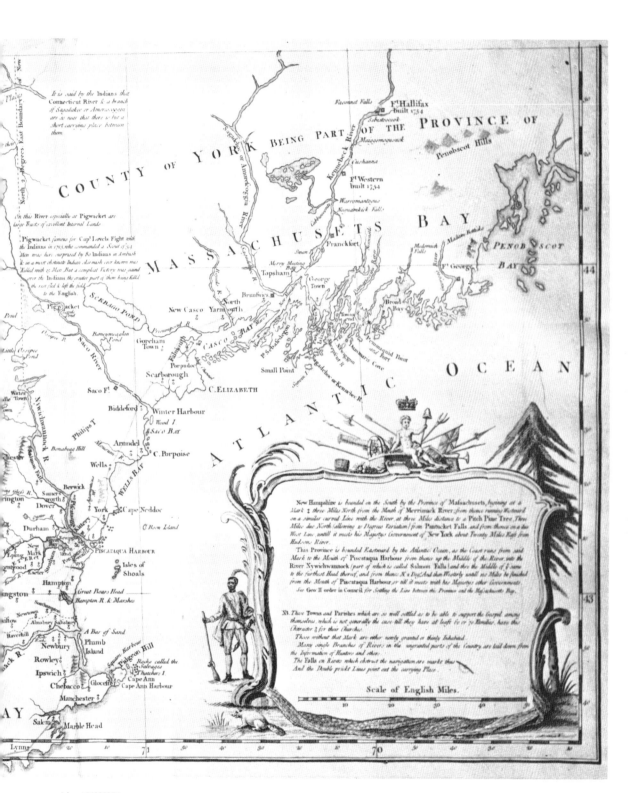

shire. (NHHS)

ment;" of William Leddra on March 14, 1660, "for being a Quaker," and the punishment in 1662 of the Quakeresses Anna Coleman, Mary Tompkins, and Alice Ambrose, who, under the order of Major Waldron of Dover, were made fast to a cart's tail and drawn through the towns from Dover to Newburyport and publicly whipped upon their naked backs. The more liberal spirit in New Hampshire attracted large numbers of Quakers from Massachusetts, where persecution of the Quakers was severe and long continued. They became an important element in Dover and near-by communities. It is worthy of note that during the days when witches were being harried and even hanged in the Massachusetts Bay Colony, an old crone in Portsmouth, Goody Walford, who had been accused of being a witch, brought her defamers into court to answer for their slanderous words, and succeeded in recovering damages.

Whenever these early colonists settled a new town, however, they promptly built a church and installed a pastor. The first ministers in New Hampshire had been educated at English universities, and had a strong cultural as well as spiritual influence upon the life of the times. They brought with them valuable libraries, usually the only ones in the community. The minister was chosen by majority vote of the townspeople, and all taxpayers were assessed for his salary according to their ability to pay. The people went to church on foot or on horseback, the wife riding behind the husband on a "pillion." Every family was obliged to be represented at church on Sunday. During the hour of intermission, the farmers and mechanics gathered together to learn the important news of the week from some merchant or professional man whose opportunities for gaining information exceeded theirs.

Shipbuilding, fishing, lumbering, and the sale of pelts were the principal means of livelihood. By 1671, New Hampshire was shipping 20,000 tons of boards and staves and ten cargoes of masts yearly. Colonization in the interior was practically at a standstill. The settlement at Dunstable (now Nashua), begun in 1673, was the only one for nearly fifty years.

Although the settlers in southern New England had been involved early in war with the Indians, the inhabitants of the territory embraced within the limits of Mason's grant fortunately remained on friendly terms with the natives until after the outbreak of King Phillip's War (1675-78), during which Major Waldron made enemies even of the friendly Indians by disarming them in a sham battle at Dover.

A ROYAL PROVINCE (1679-1775)

A PART OF Massachusetts for thirty-eight years, New Hampshire became a separate royal province in 1679 through a commission issued by King Charles II empowering John Cutt of Portsmouth to be president of the Province and to govern it under the King. A council was appointed by the King and an assembly chosen by the people. Although a superior court and three

HANNAH DUSTIN, mother of twelve children, was captured by Indians in 1697, near her home in Haverhill, Massachusetts, and taken with two other captives to River Islet at Boscawen. While her captors slept, she killed and scalped ten of them before making her way to freedom. The General Court at Boston paid her a bounty of 25 pounds. 3,000 of her direct descendants comprise the Hannah Dustin/Duston Association today. (NH/DRED)

inferior courts were established, judges were removed at will by the royal governors. New Hampshire is the only New England State to have had such a royal government. Military plans began to take shape. In 1679, the first militia was organized in each of the four towns, and put to use in the wars that followed.

From 1689 to 1763, England and France declared war against each other four times, involving the English colonists each time in wars with the Indian allies of the French. The first of these was King William's War (1689-97). Indians who had first borne a grudge against Major Waldron for more than a decade murdered him in a night attack at Dover. Attacks in Salmon Falls, Exeter, Durham, Portsmouth Plains, and other places followed. It was during this war that Hannah Dustin performed her celebrated exploit near Pennacook in the vicinity of Concord.

The royal governors sent to New Hampshire by the King proved to be tyrants, and in 1698, New Hampshire, in revolt, allied itself with Massachusetts to the extent that the two provinces had the same governor. This alliance continued for forty-three years, although each province had its own legislature and council.

During Queen Anne's War (1702-13), New Hampshire was subjected again to minor Indian forays. The next conflict with the Indians is sometimes known as the Fourth Indian War (1721-25), but more often as Lovewell's War from the name of the popular hero of the conflict. This war was with the Pequawket Indians alone, and was concluded in 1725 when Captain Lovewell and his New Hampshire militia came upon some hostile Indians near Conway, New Hampshire. After the encounter, in which the intrepid Lovewell met his death, Indian hostilities were curbed for two decades.

17

CONCORD IN THE EIGHTEENTH CENTURY was little more than an armed camp. The future home of the state capital was chosen for its geographical location in the center of the state. The first capital of Portsmouth moved to Exeter, the Revolutionary capital, to avoid attack by British ships. The final move to Concord came as population shifted away from the coast and spread all over the state. Its very name means harmony, and all roads lead to it. (LML/PSC)

Fear of Indian attack, however, had hindered colonization. For many years the colonists of New Hampshire had had to fight for their homes. Indians lay in wait for them; proprietors sought to rob them of their property; kings usurped the government; famine wasted their strength; and the French hired Indians to murder them. The marvel is not that colonization was so slow, but that any settlers remained to colonize. The population in 1732, more than a century after the first settlement, was only about 12,500.

By this time frontier forts had been established in the Connecticut Valley to protect Massachusetts inhabitants to the south. Others had crossed the boundary line of Massachusetts, as it is now known, to found towns in southern New Hampshire, while a spearhead of advance had been made up the Merrimack River. Meantime, the interior, north and west of the four original towns, had begun to fill up with settlers. Towns in New Hampshire were granted to groups of individuals under charters of three types: (1) those issued under the authority of the Massachusetts Governor, commonly called Massachusetts grants; (2) those after 1741 issued by the Governor of New Hampshire; (3) Masonian charters made by the Masonian proprietors. Thirty-eight towns were chartered by 1732. The years from 1719 to 1735 saw the beginnings of four important centers. Scotch-Irish settlers, numbering one hundred and twenty Protestant families seeking to escape the religious prosecution of English kings, came to Londonderry after 1719, bringing with them the Irish potatoe and the art of spinning Irish linen. Rochester was incorporated in 1722, and the first settlement was made in 1728. Concord was settled as Penacook in 1727 and incorporated as Rumford in 1733, the name being changed to Concord in 1765. In 1735, Manchester, originally known as Harrytown, was granted by the Masonian proprietors to the "snowshoe men" of Captain William Tyng and the name changed to Tyngstown.

18

Incorporated in 1751 as Derryfield, the town was named Manchester after the English industrial city in 1810.

Industrial and commercial conditions existing in the province of New Hampshire in 1737 are thus described by the first New Hampshire historian, Jeremy Belknap:

> The traffic of the province at this time consisted chiefly in the exports of lumber and fish to Spain and Portugal and the Caribee Islands. The mast trade was wholly confined to Great Britain. In the winter small vessels went to the southern colonies with English and West Indian goods, and returned with corn and pork. The manufacture of iron within the province lay under discouragement and want of experienced and industrious workmen. Woolen manufacture was diminished and sheep were scarcer than formerly, the common land on which they used to feed being fenced in by the proprietors. The manufacture of linen was much increased by means of the emigrants from Ireland who were skilled in that business. No improvements were made in agriculture and the newly granted townships were not cultivated with the spirit of success.

The Reverend David Sutherland, of Bath, wrote at this time:

> The people in these times were a very plain people, dressing in homespun cloth. Every house had its loom and spinning-wheel, and almost every woman was a weaver. Carding-machines were just introduced at the beginning of the nineteenth century and clothiers had plenty of work. The first coat I had cost me a dollar and a half per yard, spun and woven by one of my best friends; and I know not that I ever had a better. For many years there was not a single wheeled carriage in town. People who owned horses rode them; and those who had them not went on foot. Sleighs or sleds were used in winter. I have seen ox-sleds at the meeting-house. For years we had no stoves in the meeting-house. For years we had no stoves in the meeting-house of Bath; and yet in the coldest weather, the house was always

The fact that no public execution took place in New Hampshire in more than one hundred and twenty years in evidence of the freedom from capital crime in this period. In 1740, The New Hampshire Massachusetts controversy regarding the boundary line, which had been carried on for years, was settled by a decree from the King. From 1732 to 1742, during a period of freedom from Indian warfare, the population of New Hampshire nearly doubled to 24,000, and four more small towns were established.

In 1741, New Hampshire received her first governor in her own right in the person of Benning Wentworth, and at the same time the Provincial Legislature was given increased authority. This form of government was continued until changes brought about by the Revolution. In the twenty-five years of his rule, Governor Wentworth granted more territory and established more townships than all his predecessors put together. As a result of their participation in the wars, the troops had become acquainted with the interior, and there was a scramble to obtain this land. Governor Wentworth's method of granting townships, however, was the most objectionable of his practices, and had much to do with bringing about his downfall. Distributing about two hundred tracts of land of generous proportions to various groups of persons, it was his practice in each case to reserve for himself a personally se-

19

GOVERNOR BENNING WENTWORTH, the first Royal Governor of New Hampshire (1741-1766), and scion of the state's most influential and wealthy family prior to the Revolutionary War. He granted more territory and established more townships than all his predecessors put together, at no mean profit to himself. (NHSL)

THE REVEREND JEREMY BELKNAP, minister at Dover, and New Hampshire's first historian. His three-volume *History of New Hampshire,* completed in 1792, is a classic of American regional history. It remains the most important single work relating to the early history of New Hampshire. Belknap County was named in his honor. (NHHS)

Facing page: BELKNAP'S MAP of New Hampshire, first published in 1791 as a frontispiece for volume 2 of his *History of New Hampshire.* The only change is that this map shows 960 more acres belonging to Dartmouth College in its northern New Hampshire acreage. (JB)

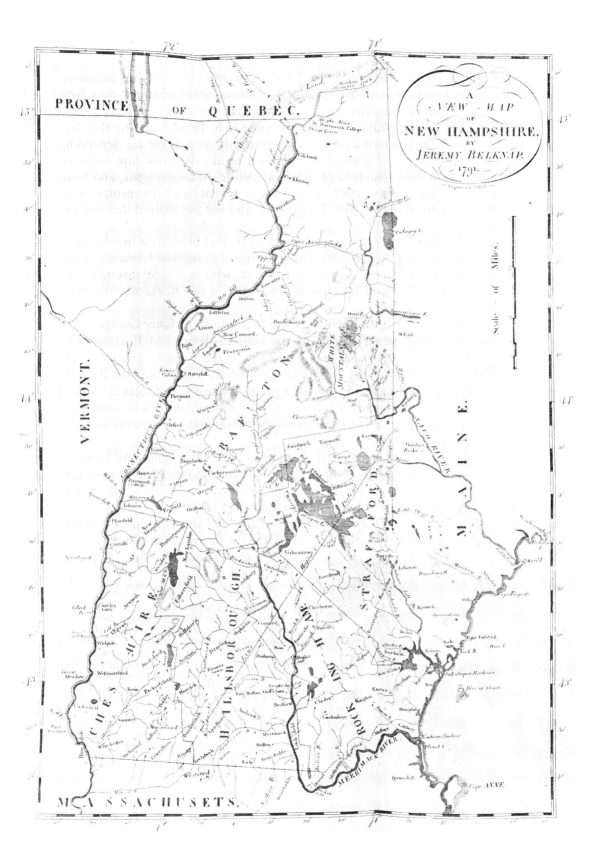

A NEW MAP OF NEW HAMPSHIRE, BY JEREMY BELKNAP. 1791.

lected lot of five hundred acres. In less than twenty years he thus acquired, without expense to himself, one hundred thousand acres scattered over New Hampshire in such a manner that in whatever the growth of population and trade might turn, he could not fail to become rich. Besides getting that five hundred acres, he received a fee for each grant, the size of the fee depending upon the capacity of the grantee to pay. As a result, the townships went for the most part to successful men of New Hampshire, Massachusetts, and Connecticut. During Wentworth's incumbency, seventy-five townships were granted or incorporated in New Hampshire, and the population increased to 52,000.

From 1734 to 1744 there was a widespread revival of interest in religion in the State, traceable to the preaching and writing of Jonathan Edwards and of the great English preacher George Whitefield, who travelled through New Hampshire. The Puritan Church was practically, if not in theory, the State Church.

When hostilities were resumed in the conflict known as King George's War (1744-49) the outstanding event was the spirited defense of Fort Number Four at Charlestown. In the last struggle with the French, known as the French and Indian War (1754-63), Captain Robert Rogers and his Rangers made a spectacular raid against the St. Francis Indians near Quebec. Around this raid has grown up many a legend. Although the frontier was constantly in a state of alarm during the Revolution, New Hampshire in reality has seen the end of Indian fighting.

Journalism and overland transportation in New Hampshire had their beginnings in the next few years. In 1756, the first newspaper, *The New Hampshire Gazette,* was printed at Portsmouth, and in 1761 the first regular stagecoach travelled between Boston and Portsmouth.

Upon the capture of Quebec and Montreal in 1759 and 1760, and the establishment of the Franco-English peace of 1763, the tide of migration into west-

MAJOR ROBERT ROGERS who led 200 of his famous rangers against the Indian hell-hole village of St. Francis on the banks of the St. Lawrence River in 1759 from Fort No. 4 in Charlestown. After a 22-day march, the rangers launched a three-pronged attack and achieved complete surprise. The sight of 600 white scalps spurred them on; the slaughter was terrible, and the rangers looted a French catholic church before burning the village flat. Pursued night and day by the infuriated Indians, the rangers buried two gold candlesticks at Memphremagog, and split up in several small parties in an attempt to reach Fort Wentworth near what is today Stratford Hollow. The gold candlesticks were found in a swamp in 1816, and legend has it that a ten-pound silver statue of the Virgin still haunts the woods near the spot where one of the retreating parties of rangers was overtaken and massacred by the Indians. The statue of the Virgin has never been found. Less than half of the original force lived to reach Fort No. 4. Rogers, a Tory at heart, died in England where he went to live during the Revolution. (NHHS)

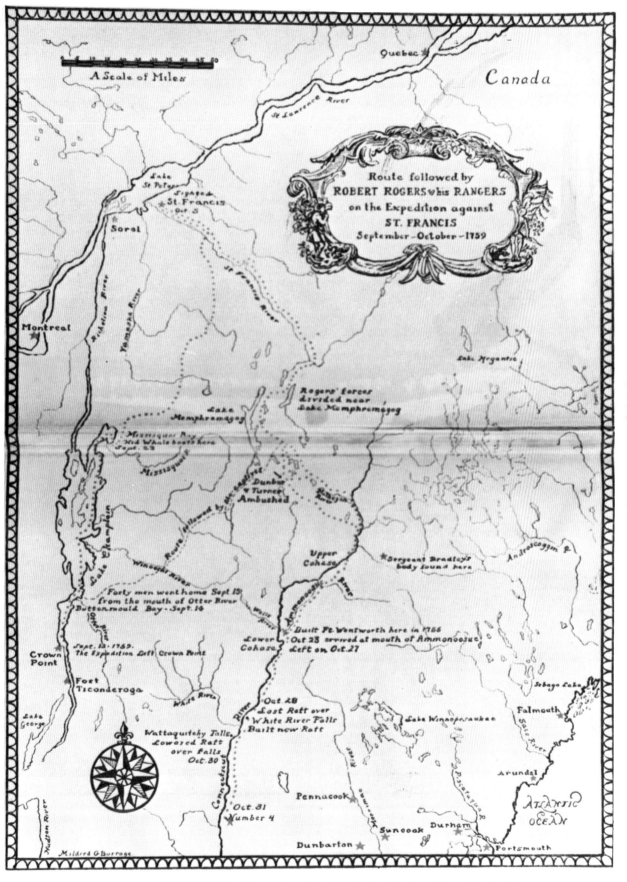

THE ROGER'S EXPEDITION MAP of the attack against the St. Francis village, September-October 1759. Roger's exploit was the subject of the 1940s film "Northwest Passage" starring Robert Young and Spencer Tracy, from the novel of the same name by Kenneth Roberts. (NHHS)

ern New Hampshire received great impetus. The broad meadows and rich soil of the Connecticut River Valley attracted many settlers, who for some years had been slowly filtering in from the settlements of the Province to the south.

The last of the Royal Governors was John Wentworth II, nephew of Benning Wentworth, who held the office from 1767 to 1775. At the time he came into power, the population of the State was 52,000, and in six years it increased forty percent. The Governor distributed grants to townships, as had his predecessor, but also undertook to build good roads from the interior to the sea. He was instrumental in interesting the Earl of Dartmouth in the founding of Dartmouth College (1769) in Hanover, and endowed it with some forty thousand acres of land. Manufacturing increased, the Governor reporting in 1768 that about twenty-five thousand yards of linen were manufactured annually.

As an aid to government, the legislature in 1769 passed an act to divide the state into five counties, Rockingham, Strafford, Hillsborough, Cheshire, and Grafton, all but Cheshire receiving the names of English noblemen who were personal friends of the Governor. The act did not go into effect until two years later.

This was a period of great public improvements that were usually financed by lotteries. The practice even entered the educational realm, for in 1773, the president of Dartmouth College petitioned the legislature to "be empowered to set up a lottery for the benefit of Dartmouth College."

The first armed resistance in New Hampshire to Great Britain occurred on December 14, 1774, when a small party captured Fort William and Mary in New Castle, and removed the powder and guns to Durham. Some of this powder was later used in the battle for Bunker Hill.

Although Wentworth had not been a bad governor, in 1775 resentment toward Great Britain became so intense that his surrender was demanded, and he left Portsmouth. To take his place a Committee of Safety was organized. This committee summoned a revolutionary assembly to meet at Exeter. Thus the first of five Provincial Congresses of New Hampshire came into authority.

On January 5, 1776, the Provincial Congress adopted a temporary constitution, drawn up in 1775, which lasted until a permanent constitution was adopted by the people nine years later. By this act, New Hampshire became an independent Colony seven months before the Declaration of Independence was signed. The brief document established a bicameral legislature, but no real executive, the president of the upper house acting in an executive capacity. Never ratified by the people, this first New Hampshire constitution was put into effect on the day of its adoption, on January 5, 1776, and lasted until June 2, 1784, during a momentous period in constitutional development in the United States.

Under this temporary constitution, the Committee of Safety was an important and necessary factor in State government. Since there was no governor, the committee was chosen from the House and Council to administer the government whenever the legislature was not in session. Three Committees of Safety were chosen by the conventions and Provincial Congresses prior to January 5, 1776, and eighteen were chosen under the temporary constitution.

The fact that civil government was maintained for nine years, including the Revolutionary War period, under a constitution so weak and imperfect, indicates that the people, though they had rebelled against the existing government, were essentially law-abiding.

On June 15, 1776, a convention of both houses adopted a Declaration of Independence that was sent to the New Hampshire delegation in Congress.

REVOLUTIONARY PERIOD (1775-1783)

AT THE BEGINNING of the Revolution, after the battles of Lexington and Concord, New Hampshire was able to rush into the field three regiments of militia fairly well trained and equipped—due, ironically enough, to the arduous efforts of Royal Governor John Wentworth, who had encouraged drilling the militia as a defense against invasion "by His Majesty's enemies." When the Continental Army was organized in June, 1775, New Hampshire's quota was fixed at three regiments, and it was a simple matter for the State to change its three militia regiments already in the field from their status as State troops to those of the Continental Army. These three regiments fought throughout the war.

Officers and men were badly fed and poorly clothed, their monthly salaries running from $6.66 for a private to $166 for a major general. Terms of enlistment of New Hampshire men in the Continental Army differed greatly and were constantly expiring. On August 18, 1780, General George Washington wrote to Chairman Meschech Weare of the New Hampshire Committee of Safety: "I am largely persuaded that the duration of the war and the greater part of the misfortunes and perplexities we have had to experience, are chiefly to be attributed to the system of temporary enlistment." As the war dragged on, various inducements were offered to get recruits. In addition to bounties of £10 each from town and State, the Continental Congress offered

GOVERNOR JOHN WENTWORTH, nephew of Benning Wentworth, and New Hampshire's last Royal Governor (1767-1775). One of the state's youngest governors, Wentworth took the oath of office as "Captain-General, chief executive and Vice-Admiral of New Hampshire." The first man to receive an honorary degree from Dartmouth, he was instrumental in starting the college. He owned one of the first summer homes in the state, and was forced from office following the attack on Fort William and Mary. His was the stormiest administration in the history of New Hampshire. (NHSL)

REVEREND ELEAZER WHEELOCK teaching the Indians. Gov. John Wentworth interested the second Earl of Dartmouth in the school, and saw that its charter was granted by the provincial legislature in 1769. Wheelock's motto for the school, *vox clamantis in deserto*—"a Voice Crying in the Wilderness"—was appropriate for the chosen site on the frontier in west-central New Hampshire. (BML/DC)

a $20 bounty, 100 acres of land, and a suit of clothes. Even with this, the raising of troops became so difficult that in 1779 the State Legislature enacted the initial Draft Law.

Out of approximately 18,000 men of fighting age in New Hampshire, the largest number to render military service at any one time was about 4000. The greater part of the real fighting was done by a small nucleus, varying from 1000 to 2500 in the First, Second, and Third New Hampshire Regiments of the Continental Army. These regiments played an important part in winning the war. They contributed to the repulse of the British at Bunker Hill, marched with Sullivan's ill-fated Canadian expedition, formed the right wing at Trenton, followed Arnold in his charge at Saratoga, starved and shivered at Valley Forge, were present at the surrender of Yorktown, and watched the British evacuate New York. When the war was over, the First New Hampshire Regiment had served continuously for a period of eight years and eight months, probably the longest service record of any Revolutionary regiment.

During the war, about three thousand New Hampshire men were engaged in privateering, preying upon unarmed British merchantmen or the supply ships of the British Army, and receiving liberal rewards for the risks they took. After 1776, about one hundred small privateers of eight or ten guns were operating out of Portsmouth. They cruised along the American coast from Nova Scotia to the West Indies, and even carried their activities into the mid-Atlantic, the English Channel, and the North Sea. One Portsmouth privateer did not hesitate to sail into the mouth of the Garonne River in France, to capture a British merchantman.

The commanding officer of the Portsmouth privateer *General Sullivan* received £36,793 as his share of a single prize in 1780, not an unusual amount. The share of ordinary seamen on the same privateer amounted to about £2500. Many of the men were captured, impressed into the British Navy, or

26

FORT WILLIAM AND MARY was the scene of the first organized fight of the Revolutionary War. Built shortly after 1623 to protect Portsmouth harbor, it was remodeled and strengthened during the reign of William and Mary and named in their honor. Alerted by Paul Revere in his first public ride, a group of New Hampshire patriots under the command of Capt. John Langdon and Major John Sullivan led the assault and captured the fort, removing the guns and powder to deny them to the British. The first overt act against the crown, this attack made war inevitable. The fort was re-named Fort Constitution, and the guns and 100 barrels of powder were used at Bunker Hill. (NHP)

imprisoned in foul jails. These privateers risked being hung as pirates while they struck unceasingly at Britain's vital trade. In 1778, Dr. Josiah Bartlett of Kingston, New Hampshire, wrote:

> I think experience has shown that privateers have done more to distressing the trade of our enemies, and furnishing these states with necessaries, than Continental ships of the same force; and that is in my opinion the greatest advantage we can at present expect from our Navy; for at this period we cannot expect to have a Navy to cope with the British.

Three Continental naval vessels were constructed at the Portsmouth shipyards during the Revolution—the *Raleigh,* the *America,* and the *Ranger,* the latter commanded by John Paul Jones, and the first warship to carry an American flag, the one made by Betsy Ross.

New Hampshire was the only State of the original thirteen that was not invaded by the British forces during the Revolution.

From the time Vermont became an independent State in 1777 until 1782, New Hampshire was in constant trouble with its neighbor over the dividing line between them. A large number of towns that had previously been and are now included in New Hampshire desired to cast in their lot with Vermont. However, acting under pressure from General George Washington in 1782, the Vermont Assembly dissolved the union of thirty-four New Hampshire towns with Vermont, and they returned to New Hampshire. They demanded a representative from each town, resulting in a situation that obtains and accounts for the large size of the present legislature.

The period from 1778 to 1783 was one of constitutional change. Since the constitution of 1776 was avowedly temporary, delegates met in 1778 to devise a permanent organic law. This proposed constitution, when presented to

27

Province of N E W - H A M P S H I R E

A PROCLAMATION,
BY THE GOVERNOR.

WHEREAS feveral Bodies of Men did, in the Day Time of the 14th, and in the Night of the 15th of this Inftant December, in the moft daring and rebellious Manner inveft, attack, and forcibly enter into His Majefty's Caftle William and Mary in this Province, and overpowering and confining the Captain and Garrifon, did, befides committing many treafonable Infults and Outrages, break open the Magazine of faid Caftle and plunder it of above One hundred Barrels of Gunpowder, with upwards of fixty Stand of fmall Arms, and did alfo force from the Ramparts of faid Caftle and carry off fixteen Pieces of Cannon, and other military Stores, in open Hoftility and direct Oppugnation of His Majefty's Government, and in the moft atrocious Contempt of his Crown and Dignity ;----

I Do, by Advice and Confent of His Majefty's Council, iffue this Proclamation, ordering and requiring, in his Majefty's Name, all Magiftrates and other Officers, whether Civil or Military, as they regard their Duty to the KING and the Tenor of the Oaths they have folemnly taken and fubfcribed, to exert themfelves in detecting and fecuring in fome of his Majefty's Goals in this province the faid Offenders, in Order to their being brought to condign punifhment ; And from Motives of Duty to the King and Regard to the Welfare of the good People of this Province : I do in the moft earneft and folemn Manner, exhort and injoin you, his Majefty's liege Subjects of this Government, to beware of fuffering yourfelves to be feduced by the falfe Arts or Menaces of abandoned Men, to abet, protect, or fcreen from Juftice any of the faid high handed Offenders, or to withhold or fecrete his Majefty's Munition forcibly taken from his Caftle ; but that each and every of you will ufe your utmoft Endeavours to detect and difcover the Perpetrators of thefe Crimes to the civil Magiftrate, and affift in fecuring and bringing them to Juftice, and in recovering the King's Munition; This Injunction it is my bounden Duty to lay ftrictly upon you, and to require your Obedience thereto, as you value individually your Faith and Allegiance to his Majefty, as you wifh to preferve that Reputation to the Province in general ; and as you would avert the dreadful but moft certain Confequences of a contrary Conduct to yourfelves and Pofterity.

GIVEN at the Council-Chamber in Portfmouth, the 26th Day of December, in the 15th Year of the Reign of our Sovereign Lord GEORGE the Third, by the Grace of GOD, of Great-Britain, France and Ireland, KING, Defender of the Faith, &c. and in the Year of our Lord CHRIST, 1774.

By His EXCELLENCY's Command,
with Advice of Council.

J. WENTWORTH.

Theodore Atkinfon, Sec^{ry}.

GOD SAVE THE KING.

THE WENTWORTH PROCLAMATION ordered the arrest and punishment of those engaged in the raid on Fort William and Mary, and warned the people against being seduced from their allegiance "by the false arts or menaces of abandoned men." The people's sympathies were with the assailants of the fort, and there was never any danger of their arrest. (NHHS)

A LIST of the Soldiers who have deserted from the three New Hampshire Battalions, in the Continental Service.

Name	Place	Name	Place	Name	Place
THOMAS LOW, of Pennsylvania.		Daniel Bain,		Newbury-Port.	Samuel Ash,	Newtown.
Matthew Winfield. Ditto.		Hix Small,		Cape-Cod.	Ebenezer Judkins,	Brintwood.
Peter Hanes,	Providence.	John Kelly,		Nottingham.	Jonathan Jennes,	Mitchel.
John Finley,	Marblehead.	James Wail,			John Sanborn,	Kensinton.
William Shaw.		Thomas M'Loy,		Portsmouth.	John Fot.	Newbury-Port.
John Raine,	New-Britain.	John Yeoman,		New-Ippwich.	Thomas Holmes,	Otter-Creek.
Johnson Smith,	New-Boston.	Asa Holt,		Hartford	Daniel Chandler,	Concord.
Thomas Hammon,		Samuel Harper,		Ackworth.	Charles Hacket,	Tumworth.
Michael Lasey.		Thomas Harpet		Ditto.	James Gorden,	Epping.
Matthew Holcomb,	Boscawin.	John Harper,		Ditto.	Charles Brignt.	
John Lawrey,	Litchfield.	Elkiah Froit,		New Jersey.	John Ayers,	Londonderry.
Simon Nowles,	Brintwood.	John Baldwin,		Hanover.	Prat Chase,	Concord.
Phillip Judkins,	Unity.	William Page.			Thomas Adams,	
Thomas Johnton,	Walpole.	Christopher Billings,		Hartford.	Thomas Berry,	
Joseph Goffe,	Waterbury.	Seth Rice,		Chester.	Richard Emerson,	Haverhill.
Thomas Wheeler,	Malden.	George Hogg,		Dunbarton.	Paul Wells,	Rumney.
Reuben Thorn.		John Reams,		Chester.	John Burton,	
James Chesley,	Durham.	Joseph Frost,		Ditto.	John Martin,	Goffestown.
Edward Thomas,	New-York.	James Randlet,		Exeter.	Isaac Gay.	
James Hooper,	Ditto.	Jeremiah Robinson,		Epping.	John Wilson.	
John Gardner,	Canterbook.	George Yeaton,		Portsmouth.	John Bradshaw.	
David Thompson,	Chesterfield.	Thomas Pace,		Mitchel.	Francis Carr,	
Thomas Smith,	Worcester.	Oliver Beacon,		Rindge.	John M'Dornan.	
James Parker,	Taunton.	Daniel Russel,		Ditto.	Nathaniel Chase,	Salem.
William Allds,	Merrimack.	Samuel Witten,		Ditto.	John Wooley,	Winchester.
Edward Robinson	New York.	Daniel M'Carte.			Samuel Britain,	Westmoreland.
John Robinton,	Halsstown.	John Edwards.			Levi Fuller,	Chesterfield.
John Willey, Charlestown, No. four.		James Patten.			Caleb Aldridge,	Westmoreland.
John Smith,	Ditto.	Abraham Clifford,		Rye.	William Goody,	New-Castle.
James Thomas,	Piermont.	Asa Knowlton,		Epsom.	Samuel Colk,	Casco-Bay.
William Wheeler.		Aaron Hale,		Dunbarton.	Ezpuros Reed,	New-Salem.
William Sharper.		Caleb Hunt		Dubin.	William Young,	Dover.
John Taylor,	Amberst.	John Swan,		Ditto.	Daniel Clarke,	New-Castle.
Ebenezer Barker,	Dover.	Thomas Parks.			Robert Bragg,	Isle of Shoals.
David Hill,	Candia.	John Colkin,		Brattleborough.	Nathan Fith	Mason.
Duncan Campbell.		James Sloyn,		New-York.	Joseph Costo	
Nehemiah Eastman.		Duncan Cambell,		Boston.	Joseph Gilbartelmey	
James Goodwin.		Robert M'Knight,		Derrsfield.	Corporal Tripp	
Joseph Smith,	Boston.	John Rawlins,		Greenland.	Jack Honnaway	
Benjamin Eker.		Gideon Glitton,		Lee.	Matthew Witherinton	
Edward Smith,	Portsmouth.	Matthias Welch,		Nottingham.	John Talvor	
James Aikin,	Chester.	William Griffin,		Portsmouth.	Charles Vorton	
Robert Holland,	Newmarket.	Matthew Mallom,		Great-Island.	Matthew Gotey	
William Frazer,	Pembroke.	John Elleson,		Ditto.	Antoney Barber	
Moses Perry,	Portsmouth.	Benja Hicks,		Nottingham.	Bartelmey Cobey	
Daniel Daily.		John Stapels,		Dover.	John Row	
Andrew M'Donald.		David Batcheldor,		Raymond.	Luas Devinow	
James Eastman.		Samuel Smith,		Gilmantown.	Venson Anastas	
John Powell,		Enos Jewell,	Exeter.	Unity.	Joseph Chartard	

STATE OF NEW-HAMPSHIRE.

In COMMITTEE of SAFETY, Exeter, July 23, 1779.

ALL Officers, Civil and Military, in this State, are required ; and all others Persons, who have the Good of their Country at Heart, are earnestly requested (without Delay) to apprehend, and properly secure in some Goal in this State, any, and all the above Deserters ; and to give Notice to the Committee of Safety ; for which Service a reasonable Allowance will be made.

M. WEARE, President.

THE COMMITTEE OF SAFETY ruled New Hampshire throughout the entire period of the Revolutionary War. Its members were chosen from the House and Council to administer the government whenever the legislature was not in session. It effectively took the place of a governor. This particular document pertains to desertions in the three New Hampshire Battalions, and is signed by Meshech Weare, the first President of the first state to adopt a Constitution in the United States. (NHP)

the people for ratification in 1779 at their town meetings, was found to have so many deficiencies that it was rejected almost unanimously. Another constitutional convention was appointed that had no less than nine sessions and continued for more than two years. Three constitutions were submitted to the people before a satisfactory document was accepted in 1784. Nineteen towns, including several in the western part of the State that preferred to belong to Vermont, did not send delegates to the convention.

Objections to the constitution proposed in 1781, which divided the government into three branches, legislative, executive, and judicial, centered around (1) a stipulation that a person must own property to be a voter, and (2) the suggested method of electing the House of Representatives, which the people felt gave undue political influence to the older towns in the State. In 1782, the constitution was again presented. Several changes had been made, including the abolition of property qualifications and provision for the election of representatives by towns, with every incorporated town of one hundred and fifty voters having the privilege of choosing one representative.

This second plan was generally approved, but was not completed at the time the news of peace arrived, so the old Constitution of 1776 was revived for another year. In the following autumn the new one was finished, and was declared to be "the civil constitution for the State of New Hampshire" on June 2, 1784. The title of "governor," too reminiscent of royal rule, had been changed to "president."

This document, modeled on the celebrated Massachusetts constitution of 1780, is prefaced by a bill of rights of thirty-eight articles, roughly parallel to the first ten amendments to the Federal Constitution, but asserting the right of revolution (Article 10). Such fundamentals as freedom of the press and the right of petition and assembly are guaranteed. The functions of the legislative, executive, and judicial branches are clearly defined.

After the adoption of the constitution, political activity began to take shape in the two-party system.

PERIOD OF EXPANSION (1783-1900)

DURING THE YEARS immediately following the Revolution, the young State prospered greatly. Roads, turnpikes, mills, and factories were built, and schools, academies, scientific and religious societies multiplied. Phillips Exeter Academy was founded in 1781, and in 1791 academies at Atkinson and Amherst were incorporated. The New Hampshire Medical Society, one of the oldest organizations of its kind in America, was incorporated in 1791. A "social" library was incorporated in Dover in 1792, and in the same year the first bank was established at Portsmouth. In 1793, seventeen years before Fulton, a steamboat was launched at Orford on the Connecticut River. In 1796, the first New Hampshire Turnpike, from Portsmouth to Penacook

JOHN LANGDON, a delegate to the second Continental Congress from Portsmouth, became New Hampshire's second chief executive. As President pro tempore of the First United States Congress, he administered the oath of office to President George Washington. (NHSL)

(now Concord), was incorporated. In 1798, a Medical School was founded in connection with Dartmouth College.

New Hampshire was the ninth State to adopt the Federal Constitution. The vote, taken at Concord on June 21, 1788, was close (57 to 46) and important, for with ratification by New Hampshire the Constitution became operative throughout the Confederation. New Hampshire's first Congressmen (1789) were Senators John Langdon (president *pro tempore* of the First United States Congress) and Paine Wingate, and Representatives Abiel Foster, Nicholas Gilman, and Samuel Livermore.

The opening of the nineteenth century found New Hampshire with a population of 183,858, well scattered over the State. Agriculture, lumbering, and fishing were the principal industries. Small water-powers were being utilized for sawmills and gristmills, but as yet there was no demand for or development of the great water-powers of the State. The first cotton-goods factory in New Hampshire was built at New Ipswich in 1803, deriving its power from the Souhegan River.

The farmer of this period lived upon the produce of his own soil and clothed himself in wool from his own sheep. Trade was carried on chiefly by barter. The mechanic was not only the helper of the farmer but his peer, as his work had high value in this heyday of handicraft. Town life centered around the church and the schoolhouse.

The primitive log houses, dark, dirty, and dismal, rarely outlived their first occupants. More permanent houses were needed. The first frame houses were small, low, and cold. The windows were small, without blinds or shutters. The fireplace, however, was sufficiently large to burn logs three and four feet in length, and was built with an oven in the back. The furniture, all made of wood from native trees, was simple and useful. Pine, birch, cherry, walnut, and curled maple were most frequently chosen by the cabinetmaker. Vessels of iron, copper, and tin were used in cooking.

In *The New Hampshire Patriot* in 1821, a writer thus described the life of the period:

Farmers hired their help for nine or ten dollars a month—some clothing and the rest cash. Carpenters' wages, one dollar a day; journeymen carpenters, fifteen dollars a month; and apprentices to serve six or seven years, had ten dollars the first year, twenty the second, and so on, and to clothe themselves. Breakfast generally consisted of potatoes roasted in the ashes, a "bannock" made of meal and water and baked on a maple chip set before the fire. Pork was plenty. If "'hash" was had for breakfast, all ate from the platter, without plates or table-spread. Apprentices and farm boys had for supper a bowl of scalded milk and a brown crust, or bean porridge, or "pop-robbin." There was no such thing as tumblers, nor were they asked if they would have tea or coffee; it was 'Please pass the mug.'

Traveling was difficult. Books were few. Newspapers and letters were rare. News from England did not reach the inland towns until many weeks after the occurrence of the events reported. News from New York traveled an entire week before it reached New Hampshire.

The seat of government, which had been at Portsmouth for a century, was permanently situated at Concord in 1808. A State prison was built there in 1812, and in 1816 a State House or Capitol. The State House, twice remodeled, is still in use, but a new State prison replaced the old one in 1880.

When the second war with England (1812-15) broke out, Governor John Langdon drafted 35,000 men at the request of the President. The State militia at that time was in its most flourishing condition, and consisted of three divisions, six brigades, and thirty-seven regiments. Fourteen privateers operated out of Portsmouth.

In 1815, the celebrated Dartmouth College controversy arose when the trustees of the college tried to fire its president. Concerned about the rights of educational institutions and the inviolability of contracts, Daniel Webster argued the case brilliantly (and won) before the United States Supreme Court. The Religious Toleration Act, passed in 1819, ruled that sects not in the Congregationalist fold could no longer be taxed locally to support an institution that they had renounced.

The need of public libraries was beginning to be felt. In 1822, the first free library in New Hampshire was established at Dublin, and was followed ten

THE DARTMOUTH COLLEGE LOTTERY ticket symbolizes the many New Hampshire lotteries that have been used through the years to support education and road building. The first lottery in the state built the first glass factory at Temple. Present-day sweepstakes earnings are used solely for public education. (BML/DC)

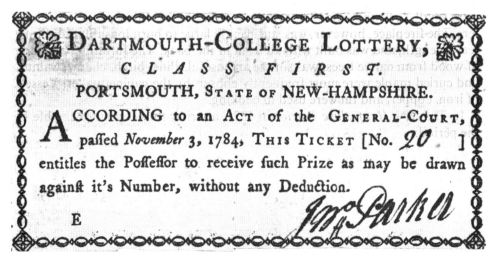

GENERAL JOHN STARK commanded a regiment of New Hampshire militia at Bunker Hill, where nearly all the troops who did the actual fighting were from New Hampshire (a fact not mentioned by any of the orators at the 150th celebration in 1925!) In 1777, he led New Hampshire soldiers in the first raising of the Stars and Stripes near Bennington, Vermont, when his New England states command won the decisive battle of the war. The Continental Congress had ordained the new flag should contain thirteen red and white stripes, with a circle of thirteen white stars on a field of blue. An exact replica is raised on a special staff in State House Plaza each April 19 and August 16. Stark's memory is honored by a statue in the State House Plaza, by the town of Stark, and by the state motto, "Live Free or Die." (NHSL)

DR. JOSIAH BARTLETT of Kingston was the second signer of the Declaration of Independence, just after the president of the Congress wrote his John Hancock large enough for King George to read without spectacles. Destined to become the first Governor of New Hampshire, Bartlett as a doctor prescribed cider in fever cases, and though his rivals accused him of malpractice, his cures made him a leader in his profession. (NHHS)

33

CAPT. JOHN PAUL JONES, the daring and celebrated naval commander, sailed early in the war from his home in Portsmouth, in the *Ranger,* a privateer of that port, destined to act against the British commerce. He landed both in England and Scotland, and plundered the house of the Earl of Selkirk. After landing his plunder in France, he challenged the British man-of-war *Drake* and fought an hour-and-a-half battle which left the *Drake* with 180 dead to his 20. After this victory, Jones left the *Ranger* for another ship, *Bonne Homme Richard,* in which his exploits rendered him the terror of the British seas. (NHSL)

GEORGE WASHINGTON visited New Hampshire in October, 1789, and was accorded the biggest welcome of any state. 700 troops under the command of General John Sullivan, dressed in brilliant red and white uniforms, greeted him at the Massachusetts-New Hampshire line. Portsmouth school children wore hats with a diamond shaped cockade and a quill; bells rang; horns and trumpets from the ships in the harbor sounded throughout the town which swelled with cheering. A Portsmouth native, Tobias Lear, was his personal secretary, and to the tune of "God Save the King," the children serenaded him:

> *"Long may thy trumpet, fame,*
> *let echoe waft the Name*
> *of WASHINGTON!*
>
> *O'er all the world around,*
> *far as earth's utmost bound,*
> *thy equal is not found,*
> *Columbia's Son."*

(From a commemorative mug—NHP)

years later at Peterborough by the first library supported by public taxation. A law passed in 1849 enabled all towns to establish and support public libraries by taxation. The State Library had its beginning in 1823, and for forty-two years thereafter the Secretary of State was the librarian. A new trend in education, based on the English public-school system, appeared when St. Paul's School was founded at Concord in 1855. At this time the Temperance and Anti-Slavery movements had their beginnings, and in 1855 the first Prohibition law was passed. It lasted until the License Act of 1903.

In 1819, the use of the power loom was introduced at the Amoskeag Mills in Manchester, and thenceforth these mills developed until they became the largest of their sort in the world. The first shoe factory in New Hampshire was built at Weare in 1823. A blast furnace was put into operation at Franconia in 1811. Gold was discovered at Plainfield in the Connecticut Valley in 1854. Despite these industrial developments, agriculture continued to be the major occupation in New Hampshire; in 1830, eighty-three percent of the State's workers were still engaged in farming. A few years later (1838), with the chartering of railroads that soon reached most parts of the State, a period of great commercial development began. This led to the rapid growth of several towns that soon became chartered cities—Manchester in 1846, Portsmouth in 1849, Nashua and Concord in 1853, and Dover in 1855. To the five original counties organized in 1769 was added another, Coös County, in 1803; in 1827 Merrimack and Sullivan were organized; and in 1840 two more, Balknap and Carroll Counties. There has been no subsequent county division.

The Northeastern Boundary controversy between Great Britain and the

O Yes! O Yes!

BENJAMIN HALL of Cornish!
BENJAMIN HALL of Cornish!
mind what your relations say, and carry
your wifes, sisters child home, or you will
have a bill of COST to pay.—Hark'ee!
Brother, Benjamin, " Hear me, for I will
speak," your abuse to your sister, turning
her into the highway for crossing your will
in marrying me, after introducing me into her company—violating the agreement
made with your brother at Sutton—still
detaining her child—by slighting the addresses made to you from your relation at
Whitingham—together with my inviola-
ble promise of publishing your uncivil
usage (in a small pamphlet,) agreeable to
law and evidence, unless you give me sat-
isfaction. know ye, that if you don't settle
with your wifes mo.her, brother and sister
within one month from this date, I will
lay open your whole proceedings in this
affair, with an address to the Judges of
Law and good breeding in this county,
wishing you to save me the trouble, and
yourself the disgrace, I subscribe myself
your affectionate brother in law.

AMOS TAYLOR.

Keene, Jan. 26, 1796.

WASHING the family laundry in public. (KPL)

MOREY'S STEAMBOAT, the first steamboat built in America, was the handiwork of Capt. Samuel Morey of Orford, who sailed it down the Connecticut River in 1792 about fourteen years before Robert Fulton invented the *Clermont*. Morey always claimed that Fulton stole his invention because Fulton came to New Hampshire and studied the Orford boat. (NHHS)

United States, which incited the Indian Stream War and resulted in setting up the Indian Stream Republic, was settled in 1842 by the Webster-Ashburton Treaty. New Hampshire came to national notice in 1852, when Franklin Pierce was elected President of the United States, the only native of the Granite State ever to hold that office.

During the Civil War (1861-65) New Hampshire sent about 39,000 men to fight for the preservation of the Union, of whom 1900 were killed in action or died of wounds, 2500 died of disease, and 285 were recorded as missing. About 1600 men re-enlisted after their first term of service. The loss of men from the Fifth New Hampshire Volunteer was greater than that from any other regiment in the Union Army; and the Thirteenth New Hampshire Regiment had the honor of leading the Union soldiers into the evacuated Confederate capital, Richmond, when the Confederacy was finally overcome.

New Hampshire's share in this conflict was such a drain upon her resources that in the decade from 1860 to 1870 her population decreased 2.5 per cent, from 326,073 to 318,300—the only decade in the State's history during which no gain was recorded. It is probable, however, that the rapid tide of emigration to the West had something to do with this decrease. Shortly afterward, improved transportation and developed water-power inaugurated a period of great industrial activity. As the impact of the Industrial Revolution began to be felt in the United States, demands for continuous water-power drew new industries to New Hampshire, where from earliest times gristmills and sawmills along a river's edge had formed the nucleus around which towns were built.

This period was notable for the transformation of towns into cities. From 1873 to 1897, six were incorporated—Keene in 1873, Rochester in 1891, Somersworth and Laconia in 1893, Franklin in 1895, and Berlin in 1897. Revision and codification of the State laws were ordered in 1865, and completed in 1867.

After the Civil War, the State began to assume more responsibility for public education. The year 1866 marked the beginning of a State university, when the New Hampshire College of Agriculture and Mechanic Arts (now a part of the University of New Hampshire) was established at Hanover. Popular education was put on a firmer basis with establishment in 1867 of a Department of Public Instruction, and since that time the State has had a universal common-school system. In 1871, the first normal school in New Hampshire was established at Plymouth, and a compulsory school-attendance law went into effect the same year.

New Hampshire's constitution, which dates from 1784, can be amended only through a constitutional convention, the citizens being called upon every seven years to vote upon the necessity of summoning such a convention. If summoned, delegates are chosen upon the same basis as members of the House of Representatives. The convention of 1876 removed the requirement that representatives, senators, and the governor "be of Protestant religion." An amendment to strike out the word "Protestant" in the Bill of Rights had been rejected by the people of New Hampshire twenty years earlier. Only twenty-one changes were made in the organic law during the century between 1792 and 1902; and even the pressures of the twentieth century have brought only slight modifications.

Public health came to the fore in 1881, when the legislature authorized the establishment of a State Board of Health. In the same year, the State Forestry Department was created, and the State began to purchase and preserve its forests.

In 1891, the legislature authorized the creation of a library commission to establish free public libraries with State aid. The New Hampshire College of Agriculture and Mechanic Arts was removed to Durham in 1893, and in the same year St. Anselm College was founded at Manchester. In 1895, the State library and supreme court buildings in Concord were dedicated.

In 1898, the war with Spain broke out, and New Hampshire sent 1358 officers and men to engage in the struggle.

THE STATE CAPITOL in Concord was built of New Hampshire granite which was dressed by convicts at the state prison. Governor Plummer laid the cornerstone in 1816, and the building was not enlarged until 1864. It is the oldest state capitol in the nation where the legislature still sits in its original chamber. (NHP)

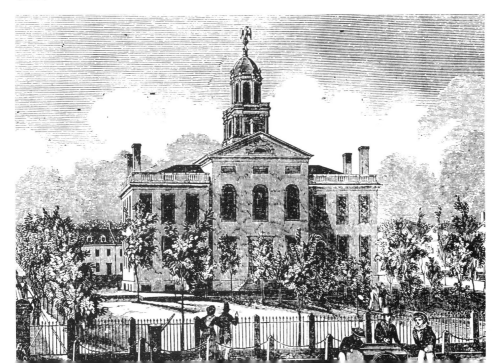

SAMUEL WILSON, known as "Uncle Sam" to distinguish him from his brother Edward, who was always called "Uncle Ned," supplied the American army with barrels of beef and pork during the war of 1812. His barrels were stamped "US" meaning that they were consigned to the government. An uninformed laborer was asked one day what the initials stood for, and he said that they stood for "Uncle Sam" Wilson. The nickname soon caught on, and to this day they refer to the embodiment of the nation. (NHP)

DANIEL WEBSTER, New Hampshire's most famous son, was one of America's most outstanding statesmen and orators. Born in Salisbury (Franklin) in 1782, he served as a congressman, senator, and twice as Secretary of State. The Dartmouth College case, in which he argued the inviolability of contracts successfully before the United States Supreme Court, established him as one of the most talented legal minds of the day. His words, "Liberty and Union, now and forever, one and inseparable," conclude one of his famous orations and represent the essence of his feelings about the United States and the Constitution.

Daniel Webster
"New Hampshire's
Greatest Son".

THE TWENTIETH CENTURY

THIS PERIOD began with many industrial and racial changes. In 1900, wage-earners in New Hampshire received an average yearly wage of $382; but from that year on, wages and the value of manufactured products increased. Corporation control of the mills first became noticeable about 1900.

With the rapid growth of factories came an influx of foreign-born workers, largely French-Canadians. By the turn of the century the percentage of foreign-born was 19.2, whereas the population had been almost entirely native in 1850 (95.2 percent). This surge of foreign-born into the State continued until the passage of the United States Immigration Act of 1924.

From 1900 onward, developments in electrical engineering made hydroelectric power a reality. Generating stations were built on the most important water-power sites, and this new energy was made available for domestic and industrial uses.

In 1901, the present judiciary system, providing for a supreme court to consider questions of law and a superior court to pass on questions of fact, was inaugurated by the legislature.

In 1905, the State Aid Road Law, by which the towns and counties were entitled to receive funds from the State to build their roads, marked a new epoch in highway development in New Hampshire. Ten years later, the improvement of highways was further assisted by the Federal Aid Road Act, whereby the Federal Government contributed fifty per cent toward the building of roads, the remainder being supplied by the State and towns.

New Hampshire came to international notice in 1905, when the Treaty of Portsmouth, terminating the Russo-Japanese War, was signed at Portsmouth.

In 1909, the Direct Primary Law, doing away with the convention system of nomination, was adopted by the legislature. In the same year, an Act of Congress known as the Weeks Bill authorized the Federal Government to acquire the White Mountain region for a National Forest. A State Department of Agriculture was established in 1913.

New Hampshire shared in the World War without stint of men or means, sending more than 20,000 men to war services, including 1869 to the Navy. The State also contributed $2,500,000 to war charities, and invested more than $80,000,000, or one-fifth of the entire wealth of the State, in government war securities. It is difficult to give an accurate account of New Hampshire men in the World War, for they served in more than one hundred different regiments scattered among many divisions. Many New Hampshire men were assigned to the Twenty-Sixth or "Yankee" Division, which suffered the losses in battle of 2130 killed and 11,325 wounded. The Portsmouth Navy Yard was an important center of shipbuilding during the war, the construction of submarines and small boats and the repairing of warships being the principal activities.

DURHAM LANDING: This scene gives little hint that in 1694 a force of about 250 Indians, under command of the French soldier de Villies, attacked settlements in this area on both sides of the Oyster River,

killing or capturing 100 settlers, and destroying 5 garrison houses and numerous dwellings. It was the most devastating French and Indian raid in New Hampshire during King William's war. (NHHS)

New emphasis on public education came in 1919 with passage of a law providing for a powerful State Board of Education, composed of educational laymen, with a professional educator serving as State Commissioner of Education.

From 1920 to 1930, while the population of New England as a whole diminished 2.6 percent and that of the United States increased only 1.2 percent, the population of New Hampshire increased 3.1 percent—from 443,028 in 1920 to 465,293 in 1930.

In 1923, the New Hampshire College of Agriculture and Mechanic Arts at Durham was incorporated as the University of New Hampshire, and was reorganized with three colleges—Liberal Arts, Technology, and Agriculture.

In 1922, the greatest strike in New Hampshire history occurred, involving the textile trades in a controversy that lasted nine months.

During the depression years of 1929 to 1936, New Hampshire suffered with the rest of the country, the industrial centers being especially hard hit. As a demand for manufactured goods fell off, great industrial plants cut down the number of their employees and in many cases shut down entirely. In Hillsborough County alone, the cotton industries lost 110,000 spindles during the year 1934-35. Outside the industrial centers, the depression was not felt so strongly. There was a noticeable return of people from the metropolitan centers to the farms and small towns. Many of those who had left the homes of their forefathers were forced to come back when they had lost their positions elsewhere.

The extensive floods in March, 1936, caused the greatest damage of any in New Hampshire's history. Hundreds of families were rendered homeless, mills and factories were closed, and bridges went down like kindling before the raging rivers. Damage to public and private property amounted to more than $7,000,000.

By the close of 1936, conditions in the State were once more definitely on the up-grade. In the great industrial centers, mills that had been idle for several years were again running full time. In Manchester the great Amoskeag textile mills had been taken over to some extent by a number of smaller concerns making a variety of products.

Yesterday's New Hampshire

ABRAHAM LINCOLN's visit to New Hampshire in 1858, and his appearances in Concord, Manchester, Dover, and Exeter profoundly influenced his politial future. He came to the state as a loving father concerned about his son Robert's progress at Phillip's Exeter Academy, and left perhaps thinking for the first time that he could be nominated for the presidency. His New Hampshire speeches made a deep impression upon the Republicans of the state, and his appeal to the Douglas Democrats was irresistible. The theme of his New Hampshire speeches was that slavery was like a black snake in bed with the children, and the problem was how to kill the snake without hurting the children. On the first ballot at Chicago, New Hampshire cast 7 votes for Lincoln, one each for Salmon P. Chase, John C. Fremont, and William H. Seward. On the next ballot, all ten were given to Lincoln, and he went on to beat Douglas and become the nation's 16th President.

SENATOR JOHN P. HALE was the foremost Abolitionist in the nation. Elected to Congress as a Free-Soiler—the only one in Congress—he earned high praise from John Greenleaf Whittier for his efforts and speeches condemning the admission of Texas to the Union as a slave state. He was one of the last persons to see Lincoln on the day of the assasination. An interesting New Hampshire connection to that affair was the discovery of a photograph of Hale's daughter, Bessie, on the body of John Wilkes Booth. (NHHS)

"GOD bless New Hampshire! from her granite peaks
once more the voice of Stark and Langdon speaks.
Courage then, Northern hearts! Be firm, be true;
what one brave state hath done, can ye not also do?

—*John Greenleaf Whittier*
("The Quaker Firebrand")

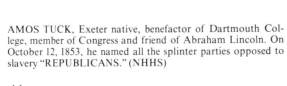

AMOS TUCK, Exeter native, benefactor of Dartmouth College, member of Congress and friend of Abraham Lincoln. On October 12, 1853, he named all the splinter parties opposed to slavery "REPUBLICANS." (NHHS)

44

THE SHAKERS of Canterbury, New Hampshire, were members of a religious sect founded by an English Quaker in 1792 who believed that perfect holiness could be attained only through physical purity and complete withdrawal from worldly pleasures. Men and women lived separately, yet together. Shaker artifacts were simple, strong, and useful. Membership was for life, and shakers were buried beneath a common stone which merely said, "Shakers." The nickname came from violent body movements during religious ecstasy. The lack of converts caused them to die out; at the height of their movement in the 1860s they numbered more than 400 in New Hampshire. They believed that the truth of their ways would never die. (NHP)

SALMON P. CHASE, a native of Lebanon, New Hampshire, was a candidate for the Republican nomination for President in 1860. As Secretary of the Treasury in Lincoln's first cabinet, he took up a suggestion from a Pennsylvania minister with Lincoln's approval: in 1864 the first coin bearing the inscription "In God We Trust" came from the mint on a 2¢ piece. Later appointed Chief Justice of the U.S. Supreme Court by Lincoln, he presided at the impeachment trial of President Andrew Johnson, at which both New Hampshire senators voted "guilty." (NHHS)

45

J. STEPHENS ABBOT (*left*) and LEWIS DOWNING (right) joined in a partnership in 1827 to build the famous "Concord coach." Abbot had been an apprentice to Massachusetts chaise builders; Downing was a wheelwright who, in 1813, advertised the opening of a shop in Concord which would sell "small wagons which he will sell as cheap as can be bought." The partnership of Abbot-Downing lasted until 1847. (NHHS)

THE CONCORD COACH was the prime achievement of Abbot and Downing who had perfected its design by 1830. In the early nineteenth century, coach design had shifted from the traditional box shape toward oval body design. From the beginning, Abbot and Downing built their carriages with flat tops to accommodate passenger luggage. What distinguished the Concord coach was its suspension system which employed "throughbraces" instead of the traditional spring-type suspension. Throughbraces were strips of leather riveted together to a thickness of about three inches, attached to run lengthwise, upon which the coach body was suspended. They gave the vehicle a swinging motion rather than the jolting up-and-down motion of the conventional springs. Mark Twain described the Concord coach as "an imposing cradle on wheels." The coaches were well-built: stout oak was used for the frame and body, the wheels cut of ash and then hand-fitted to rims and hubs. Most coaches were painted ornately, with yellow running gear and red bodies, decorated with emblems or figures. The interiors featured fine leather, polished metal, and wood paneling. (NHHS)

BUFFALO BILL driving the Deadwood Stage, a coach that figured in real-life hold-ups, and later toured with Wild West Shows. Cody drove the Deadwood Stage when it returned to Concord for the 4th-of-July celebration in 1895. (NHHS)

CONCORD COACHES going west. This trainload leaves Concord consigned to Wells Fargo. Concord coaches went all over the world; large ten-passenger coaches ended up in the diamond mines of Africa. (NHHS)

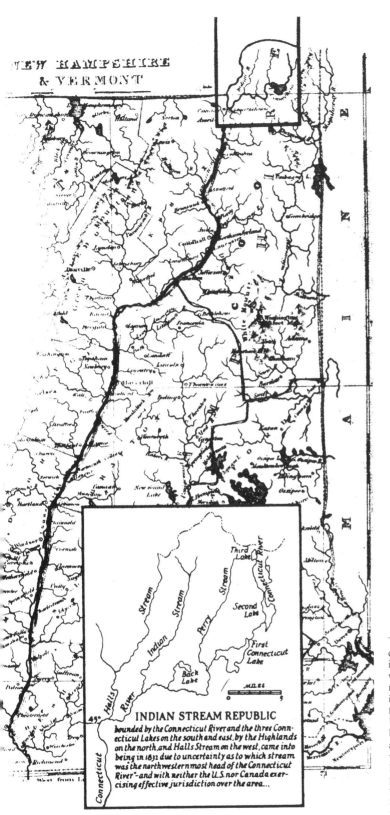

NEW HAMPSHIRE & VERMONT

Third Lake

Second Lake

First Connecticut Lake

Back Lake

Connecticut River

Indian Stream

Perry Stream

Halls River

MILES

INDIAN STREAM REPUBLIC

bounded by the Connecticut River and the three Connecticut Lakes on the south and east, by the Highlands on the north, and Halls Stream on the west, came into being in 1832 due to uncertainty as to which stream was the northwesternmost head of the Connecticut River"- and with neither the U.S. nor Canada exercising effective jurisdiction over the area...

THE INDIAN STREAM REPUBLIC constitutes one of the most extraordinary incidents in the history of the western world. The foundation of an independent republic comprising 160,000 acres in what is now the town of Pittsburg stemmed from a long-standing dispute between the United States and Canada over the boundary line between New Hampshire and the Province of Quebec. This dispute was submitted to the King of the Netherlands as the arbiter, but involved kidnapping, violence, and open warfare before it was finally settled in 1842. The Indian Stream Republic existed independently for 69 years.

NATHANIEL HAWTHORNE was New Hampshire's first publicist. He was much taken by the beauty of the White Mountains, and his stories, such as "The Great Stone Face," and "The Unexpected Guest" helped spread their fame. He and Franklin Pierce were devoted friends—Hawthorne wrote a flattering life story of Pierce for the Presidential campaign—and the two were traveling together back to the White Mountains when Hawthorne died in Plymouth's Pemigewasset House. (NHHS)

THE OLD MAN OF THE MOUNTAINS from an 1878 stereopticon view by the Kilburn brothers of Littleton. View was taken a bit too far to the north to catch the sharpest features, but may have been done so to show clearly the two people holding hands on the head. Hawthorne's story, "The Great Stone Face," and the Kilburn brothers stereopticon views of the White Mountains spread the fame of New Hampshire's natural beauty. (NHHS)

CRAWFORD NOTCH was discovered in 1771 by Timothy Nash, a Lancaster pioneer who, trailing a moose up one of the ravines, noticed an old Indian trail. The notch is named after the Abel Crawford family who guided tourists through a scenic grandeur rarely equalled in the world. The Crawfords ran the first inn of this region; cut the first trail to the summit of Mount Washington; and pioneered in opening the White Mountains to the public. The 10th New Hampshire turnpike thrust through the notch northward to connect Coös County with the seaports where local products such as potash, pelts, and assorted dairy products were exchanged for assorted loads of merchandise from Portland and points south. (NHP)

THE FRANCONIA RANGE and the Pemigewasset River as seen from Woodstock. Nathaniel Hawthorne was a frequent visitor, and was heading for the White Mountains when he died in Plymouth. (NH/DRED)

THE OLD WILLEY HOUSE in Crawford Notch (built by Abel Crawford) was witness to the famous "Willey Slide," immortalized by Hawthorne in "The Unexpected Guest." On the night of August 28, 1825, under a sky of threatening black clouds, a half-mile portion of the mountain behind the house rushed into the valley like an avalanche, with a roar that could be heard for twenty miles. Samuel Willey, his wife and five children, and two hired hands ran for a nearby shelter. Miraculously, the mountain slide split just above the house, surged by at roof-top level, and re-united below the house. The nine inhabitants of the house were swept to their deaths, but the house survived intact. Two horses were killed, but two oxen survived and were dug out later. An open bible lay on a table inside the house. The picture below shows the Willey House before the landslide. (NHP)

51

FRANKLIN PIERCE, the 14th President of the United States, was one of the more tragic figures in New Hampshire history. In state politics, he was considered a rising man; the Kennedys of his day would have been known as Massachusetts Pierces. Following his service in both houses of the U. S. Congress, he enlisted in the army and quickly rose to Major-General in the Mexican War. In 1852, he was elected President of the United States, carrying all but 4 states, and the nearest of being unanimously elected by the Electorial College of any President except Washington and Monroe. His administration was plagued by conflicts concerning slavery. He was accused of Southern sympathies, and the entire pandora's box was re-opened when he signed the bill repealing the Missouri Compromise. "Bloody Kansas" resulted, and the slavery question completely engulfed him. Pierce retired to Concord where he spent the remainder of his life burdened by numerous domestic afflictions. It was not until 1914, after Republican dominance in New Hampshire had been broken for the first time since the Civil War, that a statue of the state's only President was unveiled in State House Plaza. (NHHS)

MRS. FRANKLIN PIERCE AND SON. The former Jane Appleton of Hampton, Mrs. Pierce was so profoundly affected by the accidental death of her son Benjamin between her husband's election and inauguration that she was forced into retirement and never participated in White House Social functions during President Pierce's term. The couple had earlier lost two other sons in infancy. (NHHS)

CAMPAIGN POSTER for Franklin Pierce of New Hampshire, and his running mate, William King of Alabama. (NHHS)

THE COG RAILROAD was invented by Sylvester Marsh of Campton, who built the Mount Washington Railroad. Completed in 1869 for $39,500.00, the cog-wheel-inclined railway system climbs more than 3 miles up Mount Washington. The average grade to the 6,293-foot summit is one foot in four. Made safe by toothed wheel-and-ratchet, it is the second steepest in the world, and the first of its type. The picture looks Northeast over the Presidential Range toward the Great Gulf. (NH/DRED)

OLD PEPPERSASS, the first mountain-going locomotive, was built by Campbell and Whittier of Boston, shipped to Littleton, and then hauled piecemeal by oxen the 25 miles to Mount Washington. It was nicknamed "Peppersass" for its resemblance to an old-fashioned peppersauce cruet. The "bottle," or boiler, with its flared smokestack, was mounted on trunnions to keep it vertical regardless of grade. The locomotive had no cab and only a single pair of cylinders. A wood-burner, it was designed with the cog-wheel in front to pull itself up the steep incline. (NHP)

THE WILDEST RIDE IN THE WORLD was being your own brakeman coming down the cog railroad on Mount Washington, as these workmen are doing. A few hardy souls made the 3-mile trip in 3 minutes! (NH/DRED)

THE PASSENGERS changed, but the sign didn't, except for the photo number. (Doug Philbrick)

56

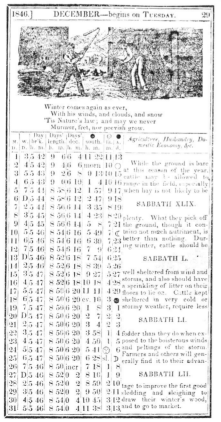

DUDLEY LEAVITT, New Hampshire's famous almanac maker born in Exeter in 1772, enjoyed only three months schooling in his entire life, but he was a self-made scholar and became one of the most celebrated teachers of his day. His interests were languages, astronomy, and mathematics. He fathered eleven children; one of his daughters was the mother of the first white child born in Minnesota. His "Leavitt's Farmer's Almanac" boasted a circulation of 30,000 by 1846. The last issue of 1852—from which this page is taken—carried a map of California "since so many of our people have gone there." (NHHS)

THE OLDEST HOUSE in Surrey was built by Peter Hayward in 1764. (NH/DRED)

It is a sadness that was always so:
always New England Places knew the doom
of having to see the hosts of children go,
of having a house to keep with too much room.

This is a cradle for the richer places,
this is a land the old ones keep and tend;
they sweep their rooms, and hope still turns their faces,
toward Spring and children at the south road's bend.

from "The Land The Old Ones Keep,"
by Robert P. Tristram Coffin

HORACE GREELEY, native of Amherst, defeated for the Presidency by General Grant, walked to New York City at the age of twenty, with $10.00 in his pocket. He struggled in publishing, and on April 10, 1841, he published the first edition of *The New York Tribune*. Elected to Congress, he lectured all over the country, and his advice "Go West, young man," was taken up and repeated millions of times. He posted the jail bond when Jefferson Davis was arrested at the end of the Civil War, and died in distressing circumstances after losing control of the newspaper he founded, and the right to edit it. (NHP)

NEW HAMPSHIRE EMIGRANTS FOR CALIFORNIA.—Thomas G. Wells, Anson Dale, Walpole;—George Hagar, Frank B. Holmes, Dr. Thomas E. Hatch, Reuben Hatch, David N. Wright, Oren Dickerson, Keene; Miles S. Buckminster, Roxbury; Dr. I. Kelley, Bristol; Thomas W. Campbell, Gilmanton; E. H. Lock, Langdon; G. K. Goodwin, Dover; Charles E. Stratton, New Ipswich; I. M. Kilton, Grafton; Edward B. McIntyre, Lancaster; B. G. Frost, Sandwich; C. Sanborn, H. T. Lyford, Barnstead; J. J. Eastman, Pittsfield; A. J. Tyrrell, William Weswell, L. Chapman, Geo. W. Janvrin, W. Derby, B. Wattles, Wm. Weymouth, Exeter; H. Sanborn, S. E. Gove, Kensington; Geo. W. Currier, Meredith; Horace Bucklin, Swanzey; Joseph Getchell, Derry.

Some six or eight have left this county for the gold regions, whose names we have not been able to obtain. We presume more than double the number reported above have left this State.

☞ Ex-Governor Paine, of Vt., is nominated as one of the Commissioners on Mexican claims.

NEW HAMPSHIRE PEOPLE headed West by the hundreds; the lure of gold and the rocky soil of New Hampshire were two good reasons. (KPL)

57

HORACE WHITE, JR., Editor-in-chief of the *Chicago Tribune,* went west from his home town of Colebrook as a member of "The New England Emigrating Company," organized by his father and fifteen other men who settled Beloit, Wisconsin, founded Beloit College, and gave that area many New England characteristics and institutions. (Chicago Tribune)

THE CLIPPER SHIP *Nightingale,* built in 1851 at the height of the Clipper ship era in Portsmouth (which lasted from 1845 to 1860), was one of the most celebrated ships built in the Piscataqua yards. She was high, narrow, beautiful and swift, for it was as important for cargo to get there fast as it was for it to get there safely. Clippers made the 90-odd-day trip around Cape Horn to the gold fields carrying everything from passengers to pianos, picks and pans. New Hampshire pride was reflected in such names of ships as *Manchester, Piscataqua, Merrimack, Granite State,* and *Chocorua.* (NHHS)

PORTSMOUTH HARBOR as seen from the Navy Yard in the 1820s. (NHP)

LAKE WINNIPEASAUKEE by Currier and Ives. New Hampshire's largest lake's name means "the smile of the Great Spirit." The lake is 20 miles long, 12 miles wide, and contains 274 islands. (NH/DRED)

THE STEAMBOAT ERA began on Lake Winnipeasaukee in 1849 when railroad interests began to promote lake travel aggressively. The *Lady of the Lake (above)* was launched that year by the Concord and Montreal system. Even though the Boston and Main Railroad put the rival ship *Chocorua* in service (and each ship operated in its own end of the lake) the *Lady of the Lake* was the queen of lake travel for almost fifty years, until replaced in 1893 by the *Mount Washington (below)* which was destroyed by fire in 1939, and in turn replaced by the *Mount Washington II.*

STEAM RAILROAD crossing the trestle toward Crawford Notch. The successor to the stage coach was the steam railroad, and New Hampshire pioneered in the use of steam for transportation. Following Morey's steamboat, the first steam fire engine was built by Nehemiah Bean in Gilmanton. Later, the Amoskeag fire engines would be widely known. The coming of the railroads took place in the first half of the nineteenth century; the first New Hampshire railroad was the Nashua and Lowell, chartered in 1835 and operational between the two cities in 1838. Gradually, the Boston and Maine secured practically a monopoly, and by 1900 dominated the railroad mileage in New Hampshire.

61

"THE ENFIELD" was an early wood-burning locomotive named after the town on the Northern Railroad. (NHP)

THE UNDERGROUND RAILROAD helping Southern slaves escape to Canada was strongly supported by the fiercely abolitionist people of New Hampshire. The map at left shows the various routes to freedom. Many homes still contain today a hidden space behind a stairwell or behind kitchen panels where escaped slaves could hide. (NHP)

THE SINGING HUTCHINSONS, natives of Milford, billed themselves as "a little nest of brothers with a sister in it." They composed most of their own songs, including several about New Hampshire. Their most famous surviving song, written by Abby in 1858 was "Kind Words Can Never Die," which later became "Old Soldiers Never Die." They were violently abolitionist, sang at Lincoln's second Inauguration, and later toured Europe successfully. Pictured here, from a sheet of their published music, are, left to right, Judson, Abby, John, and Asa. John was the last survivor. (BML/DC)

THE *USS Kearsarge* (named for the New Hampshire mountain) defeated the Confederate gunboat *Alabama* in the English Channel in 1864. Built at Portsmouth in 1861, this corvette or sloop-of-war was a neat, fast, steam-and-sail ship of 1030 tons, carrying 8 guns and 162 men. News of the victory was received with jubilation in the North, since the *Alabama,* the notorious and most-hated of the commerce raiders, had destroyed 58 ships with cargoes valued at six and one-half million dollars. England, which supported the Confederacy, received with great honor the few survivors of the *Alabama* who had escaped capture. (NHP)

63

FORT CONSTITUTION during the Civil War. (Randall)

SARAH JOSEPHA BUELL HALE of Newport was one of the earliest exponents of equal rights for women. She was the first woman to edit *Godey's Lady's Book* (the *Vogue* of its day); she helped found Vassar College; she was first to suggest public playgrounds; wrote the poem "Mary Had a Little Lamb;" and advocated and won proclamation by President Lincoln of Thanksgiving as a national holiday. (NHP)

EXECUTOR'S SALE of a horse rated a headline in 1886. (LML/PSC)

THE FARRAGUT HOTEL (seen from Little Boar's Head) was one of the great hotels from the golden era of Rye Beach. The big hotels along the coast burned and were re-built as fast as good times followed bad! (NHP)

EXECUTOR'S
SALE!
— OF —
PERSONAL PROPERTY

By virtue of a license from the Judge of Probate for the County of Grafton, the subscriber will sell at Public Auction at the dwelling house of George A. Clark, late of Plymouth, in said County, on

MONDAY, MAY 10th, 1886!

At 10 o'clock a. m., all the goods and chattels of said deceased, excepting a part of the household goods specifically bequeathed, consisting of

ONE HORSE!

Two Cows, 25 Hens, 7 Tons Hay, 14 Cords Wood, Wagon, Sleigh, Buffalo Robes, 2 horse Mower, Horse Rake, Carts, Plows, Harrows, Cultivators, Chains, Harnesses, Sugar Making Utensils, &c.   Also, lot of Household Furniture, viz: Stoves, Chairs, Tables, Bedding, Bedsteads, Crockery, &c.

☞ Conditions made known at time and place of sale.

J. H. MUDGETT, Executor.

B. F. PEASE, Auctioneer.
Plymouth, N. H., April 29, 1886.

[Democrat Print, Plymouth, N. H.

THE UNIVERSITY of New Hampshire was born in Culver Hall at Dartmouth. Picture shows a class in Civil Engineering or Surveying in 1884, when tuition was $10.00 a semester. (UNH)

PLYMOUTH NORMAL SCHOOL was the first teacher's college in New Hampshire, called a Normal School after the French "Ecole Normal" to distinguish it, presumably, from a medical or other specific type of school. Robert Frost, who taught here a short time, was remembered by some as having too many poems in his head to be much of a teacher.

TILTON PREPARATORY SCHOOL for Boys in 1888 shows an astonishing number of young ladies looking on as a row of maple trees is just being set out. Founded in 1845, Tilton is one of the northernmost prep schools in the state. Rivalry between "preppies" and "townies" developed when public secondary education came to the fore in New Hampshire. (Tilton)

THE COMPLETION of the Atlantic Cable, "The Voice beneath the Sea," was celebrated at Rye Beach in 1874. (NHP)

UNUSUAL BETS were not uncommon in the olden days. Here Mr. J. B. Fisher of Keene pays off an election bet by drawing Mr. John A. Drummer in a sulky from Central Square to the old Fair Grounds at West Keene and back, accompanied by the Keene Brass Band, a portion of the Fire Department, and, of course, a delighted crowd. (KPL)

MARY BAKER EDDY, (a native of Bow), the discoverer and founder of Christian Science, enjoyed her afternoon drives with her secretary Calvin A. Frye much more after her efforts to get Pleasant Street in Concord paved were successful. She became a legend in her own time, following the turning point in her life when she experienced a spiritual healing in 1866. She turned her lifelong study of the bible into an intensive search that produced her earliest manuscripts on Christian Science. She was convinced that Christianity was scientific in the deepest spiritual sense, and that it applied to every aspect of human experience. Constantly ridiculed and attacked by the press of the day ("A Christian Scientist is someone who sits on a hot stove and asks what's burning") her tormentors ranged from Mark Twain to Walter Dakin. As a result of life-long abuse from the press, she started *The Christian Science Monitor* and vowed never to slander or attack a person for his beliefs. The result is one of the world's greatest newspapers. (CSM)

JOSH BILLINGS sounded like a fugitive from the early days of Chautauqua—and the railroad cashed in on the act.

PRESIDENT GRANT visited the top of Mount Washington in August 1869. The Civil War hero was a frequent visitor in New Hampshire. When he found out that Jefferson Davis had once climbed Mount Washington when visiting President Pierce, Grant wanted to prove that anything a "Johnny Reb" could do, he could do as well. Yet when he proved less than successful, he called for whiskey to refresh himself, but the whiskey did not help. He finally "ascended" on a borrowed horse. In this picture, he and his party had been taken up to the summit on the new cog railway behind "Old Peppersass." New Hampshire's Henry Wilson was Vice-President under Grant. (Kilburn)

THE NEW HAMPSHIRE VETERAN'S HEADQUARTERS at the Weirs was established at the end of the Civil War, and was in the state a forerunner of the American Legion. An "encampment" was held yearly, and each regiment had its own organization and building. General Grant was a popular visitor there. (NHHS)

THE PORTSMOUTH BREWERY was the largest in New England in the 1870s, and the seventh largest in the nation. Built by Frank Jones, its nourishing stout was often recommended by doctors. Jones was a public-spirited man who dispensed a large income with a liberal hand. For many years, he was "Mr. Democrat" of the state, and just missed being elected Governor. (PPL)

THE WENTWORTH BY THE SEA, one of New Hampshire's landmark resorts, was built by Frank Jones in the mid-1880s and named for New Hampshire's first Royal Governor. It survived the fires that kept recurring in the Rye Beach area, and is a splendid reminder of what New Hampshire resorts were like in their heyday. (NHP)

AMOSKEAG MILL CHILDREN were born, brought up, educated, employed, married, and buried within the embrace of "The Textile Club," a 24-hour surveillance organization run by the New Hampshire cotton mills, the largest in the world. Mill paternalism was heavy-handed, especially with large groups of foreign immigrants. Manchester is named for the industrial town in England; Amoskeag mills owned 2500 acres on both sides of the Amoskeag river. (NHP)

DOWNTOWN CONGRESS STREET IN 1888 looked more like a small town than one of the main drags of Portsmouth. (NHP)

THE GREAT BLIZZARD of 1888 developed as a storm over the Great Lakes. Snow began to fall in New Hampshire on March 11, and never let up until March 14—three days later. More than 40 inches of snow accumulated, causing drifts twelve to fifteen feet high. Communications, transportations and all modes of life were affected for another four days. The scene here is on Elm Street in Manchester. (NHP)

A COACHING PARADE in Lancaster in 1895—proving that traffic jams existed even in "the good old days." (NHP)

SPANISH AMERICAN WAR PRISON-
ERS: Following the destruction of Admiral Cervera's fleet in Santiago Bay, the
cruiser *Saint Louis* sailed from Cuba on
July 5, 1898, with 744 prisoners, including
the Admiral himself, and 52 officers. After spending a leisurely summer in Portsmouth, they sailed on September 12th for
Santander aboard the *City of Rome*. It is
said that several of them wished to stay in
New Hampshire and make their home
here, until someone showed them a picture of a winter scene in the country!
(PPL)

THE FLUME in Franconia Notch was
one of the early attractions for which New
Hampshire became famous. (NH/DRED)

THE PROFILE HOUSE, seen from the stone which gives Cannon Mountain its name, was superbly located between two clear lakes in the heart of Franconia Notch just north of the Old Man of The Mountains. The first house opened in 1853, burned and was re-built, and burned again. This third Profile House was built by Col. Charles Greenleaf, and accommodated 500 to 600 guests. It had its share of little old ladies; when it rained, and no excursions were possible, amusement consisted mostly of sitting in the parlors and listening to hymns until someone devised the idea of bowling lumps of ice through the spacious entrance hall. On Sundays, the accepted exercise was a walk to the trestle of the Cog Railroad. The third and last Profile House burned down on August 3, 1923, sharing headlines with the startling death of President Harding. Truckload after truckload of fine furniture and elegant trappings were hauled away, supposedly for storage, but many mountain homes today are said to contain ill-gotten relics of the Profile House destruction. The cause of the fire was never determined, but in any case, the 250 foot lobby, the massive plate-glass windows draped with Irish lace, the pompeian red carpet, and the white columns and pilasters were all gone. The hapless guests straggled off to temporary quarters, notably the nearby Forest Hills Hotel. Plans to re-build were cancelled, and for $800,000 Franconia Notch became a state park in 1928, a fit successor to the vanished greatness of the old hotel. (Dick Hamilton)

75

THE IDLEWILD HOUSE in North Conway was typical of the early summer resorts which actively participated in Fourth of July festivities. Larger hotels printed special menus in red, white, and blue, featured patriotic programs, and fireworks. (NHP)

THE BOSTON AND MAINE delivered guests right to the doorsteps of the Profile House. Many of the wealthy society women brought mountains of luggage and whole retinues of personal servants. One in particular always kept a flunky complete with gold lace uniform standing guard outside her quarters. (Dick Hamilton)

THE FOREST HILLS HOTEL, seen from the north. Down the valley to the right is Franconia Village. The mountains from left to right are Lafayette, Lincoln, Haystack, Liberty, and Cannon. Below the notch are Eagle Cliffs and Bald Mountain. The Forest Hills rates took a sudden, dramatic jump the day the Profile House burned! (NH/DRED)

MOUNT WASHINGTON in early spring. Following the Civil War and the rapid growth of railroads, an increasing number of people with money and the leisure to spend it retreated to the cool mountains or the seashore of New Hampshire, and they came for the season. Hotels expanded, and new ones were built. Victorian palaces graced every mountain and valley. The 1860s ushered in a heyday of luxurious and magnificent hotels that dominated the summer vacation field, and developed a way of life that would last fifty years. The guests that thronged to fill these hotels were the rich and fashionable from the social registers of Philadelphia, New York, and Boston. A complete list of the great summer resorts would fill a small book, but some of the outstanding names are: The Wentworth, The Mount Washington, The Boar's Head, The Farragut, The Pemigewasset House, The Maplewood, The Sinclair, The Mount Pleasant, The Crawford House, The Fabyans, The Balsams—but everyone has his own list. (NH/DRED)

A LAKE TARLETON CLUB postcard was a comical example of exaggeration; most resort advertising tended to tell it like it was; postcards and postage were free in many resorts, but management was not above discarding any that contained unfavorable comments concerning the food or the service. Franconia Notch was mentioned in "Gentlemen's Agreement," the 1940s film about restricted clientele, starring Gregory Peck. (NHP)

THE WAUMBEK in Jefferson was and is known for one of the finest golf courses in New Hampshire. A short drive in any direction was rewarded by the incomparable scenery of the Presidential range. (Doug Philbrick)

CROQUET on the Monticello lawn in 1906 was one diversion, though the court seems a bit rough and you couldn't hit the ball too hard without sending it down into the next valley. (Doug Philbrick)

THE MOUNTAIN VIEW HOUSE from a Kilburn stereopticon slide shows the famous hotel in Whitefield a beehive of activity. Verandas were the rage; guests could sit and rock amid the freshest, cleanest air in the nation, and look down into the White Mountains. This is one of the finest-run hotels in the state. (Doug Philbrick)

THE TALLY-HO PARADE climaxed the social season every summer in Twin Mountain. Hotels entered gaily decorated coaches, filled with beautiful girls, and competed for lavish prizes. (Doug Philbrick)

GOLF COSTUMES were warm enough in the early 1900s; most hotels featured an easy putting green close by which saved all that walking. The round barn in the background was a thrifty way to use a lot of short timbers. (Doug Philbrick)

THE BALSAMS is New Hampshire's northernmost resort, and boasts one of the state's most spectacular views in Dixville Notch. Located halfway between Portland, Maine, and Montreal, P. Q., the hotel started as an inn on the stage route. All buildings connect underground, and it was in its heyday the most completely self-sustained resort in the state. Original plans called for five more Swiss-type buildings like the one seen in left rear that was dedicated in 1917 to the music of John Phillip Sousa. The hotel was converted in the late 1960s to a full winter-time operation in the newly-built Wilderness Ski Area. (The Balsams)

SUMMER WAITRESSES were attracted to the resorts; it meant a carefree summer with profit for school in the fall. Romances flourished, and an amazing number of New Hampshire natives worked their way through college on such summer earnings. These girls are shown in the Balsams kitchen in the late 1930s. In most summer resorts, weekly staff dances were eagerly patronized by the guests. (The Balsams)

THE PEMIGEWASSET HOUSE burns for the third and last time in the early 1950s. The famous hotel in Plymouth was one of the great landmarks of an era. Nathaniel Hawthorne died here en route to the White Mountains where he was traveling for his health with his devoted friend, Franklin Pierce. (LML/PSC)

THE MOUNT WASHINGTON HOTEL with the Presidential Range in the background. Party of hikers are returning to Fabyans and the train to North Conway after a day's outing. The International Monetary Conference was held here in 1944. Built in 1902, the Mount Washington Hotel is one of the great landmarks in the White Mountains. (NH/DRED)

81

THE ASSEMBLY HALL of the Mount Washington looking from the Ballroom toward the Banquet Hall. During the 1940s, all major hotels featured Latin dance instructors who performed nightly in the old ballrooms once used for square dancing and community sings. The Rumba and the Samba were the rage at the time. (Doug Philbrick)

82

THE TWIN MOUNTAIN HOUSE (*above*) went the way of many grand hotels when it was torn down in the early 1950s. President Grant used to stay here, and the Reverend Henry Ward Beecher (*left*) packed them in every Sunday, first in the hotel's ballroom, later in a tent, pitched nearby to accommodate the overflow crowd of the faithful who came in large numbers to hear him preach his sermons. (Doug Philbrick/Dick Hamilton)

THE DINING ROOM at the Twin Mountain House was typical of the grand service amidst festive decorations. Bell-boys rang a little silver bell on each floor to announce the opening of the dining room each evening—an unnecessary gesture since most of the guests would be lined up waiting to enter. (Doug Philbrick)

THE GLEN HOUSE was the starting point for increasing numbers of visitors who drove up the carriage road to the summit of Mount Washington as soon as it was finished in 1861. The famous hotel burned three times; the picture shows a fleet of Packards in front of the third hotel in the twenties, before it burned for the last time. (Doug Philbrick)

THE MOUNT WASHINGTON carriage road is the world's first Mountain Toll Road. It was the scene of many unusual races and endurance tests. P. T. Barnum called the view from the top of the mountain "the second greatest show on earth." The Indians thought the Great Spirit lived on the summit of the highest peak in the Northeast. The view from the summit unfolds on every side; in the south, beyond New Hampshire's lakes region and river valleys, and the Berkshires of Massachusetts; in the west lie Vermont's Green Mountains and New York's Adirondacks; and to the north is Canada. In the east is Maine, and along its broken coastline stretches the Atlantic Ocean from which this mountain top was first seen by navigators hundreds of years ago. (NHP)

84

THE ONLY NEWSPAPER printed on the summit of any mountain in the world. A copy of this unique newspaper was once printed on birch bark. Established in 1877, it was the oldest summer resort newspaper in America. Publication ceased in 1915 when the Tip Top House was destroyed by fire.

Established in 1877

The Oldest Summer Resort Newspaper in America

Among the Clouds

The Only Newspaper Printed on the Summit of any Mountain in the World

❋   ❋   Printed Twice Daily on the Summit of Mount Washington ⁑ 6,300 Feet Above the Sea   ❋   ❋

VOL XXIV.—NO. 13.   MOUNT WASHINGTON, N. H., FRIDAY, JULY 27, 1900.   PRICE 10 CENTS

THE SUMMIT HOUSE

6,300 FEET ABOVE THE SEA.

THURSDAY, JULY 26.

NOON ARRIVALS.

Mr and Mrs Gardner Knight, Boston.
J G Knight, Hanover, Mass.
Mrs A C Manson, Warsaw, N. Y.
Miss Evelyn R Manson, Warsaw, N. Y.
Miss Florence M Smith, Lynn.
Miss Nellie A Fredson,
E F Driggs, Brooklyn.
F W Driggs,   "
D B Crediford, M. D., Boston.
Miss Anna Thomas,   "
Mrs Carrie A Moore, Baltimore,
Carey A Moore,   "
Mr and Mrs H E Williams, Washington, D. C.
Miss L W Fay, Holyoke, Mass.
Miss B F Gill, Northampton, Mass.
H W Bartlett, Philadelphia.
Rev. W S M Raymond, Boston.
J G Robinson, Dover.

THE SIGNAL STATION IN WINTER.

ditions at elevated stations. We maintained stations on Mount Washington and Pike's Peak also for some 20 years after the establishment of the signal corps, and having in the 20 years' observations pretty well established the meteorological conditions at that elevation, it was thought hardly necessary to continue. There are, however, throughout the world meteorological stations,—some of them maintained by governments, a number by universities and some by private individuals,—at high elevations for the purpose of keeping a continual record of conditions at those places. There is a well equipped station maintained by British government in the north of Scotland, another at Arequipa, Peru, by Harvard University. These stations have a very general scientific purposes. But giving information for forecasting purposes they have been found not of value, because the conditions at those elevations are an indication of the probable conditions that are to follow at the surface of the earth. The pressure changes and the temperature changes to a great degree with the elevation."

THE TIP TOP HOUSE survived a great fire that swept the summit in 1908, only to burn down on August 29, 1915. It was later renovated to make it a more suitable shelter for visitors. Cables anchored in the mountain kept the building from blowing away in high winds. (Doug Philbrick)

THE HIGHEST WIND VELOCITY ever measured on earth was recorded on the summit of Mount Washington in 1934: 231 miles per hour, with gusts even higher. A man leans into the 100-miles-per-hour wind prevalent when this picture was taken—a wind that makes travel difficult and dangerous. (NHP)

THE GREAT BICYCLE CRAZE lasted from 1880 to 1918, with its peak years the decade from 1895 to 1905. Beginning in 1881, bicycle clubs sprang up all over the country, fostered by their parent organization, the League of American Wheelmen. New Hampshire registered more than 1,000 members. Whole families took to the road in Coos, Cheshire, and Rockingham counties, lunch boxes swinging from the handlebars, the entire procession moving as slowly as its slowest member. There were evening bicycle parties, meets at the fair grounds, and cross-country runs. Every town had its champion. Good riders could average sixty miles a day. Popular as the sport was, it was denounced in the First Congregational Church in Exeter by a minister who likened bicycle racers to "wild and infuriated animals let loose." The girls in this picture are from Laconia. (NHP)

DECORATION DAY, as Memorial Day is usually called in New Hampshire, always meant graveside services at the lot of the Grand Army of the Republic in the cemetery, following exercises at the Town Hall in which school children recited pieces or performed intricate patriotic drills. This observance is near the Portsmouth area in 1903. (Peter Randall)

STREET AUCTIONS on Saturday mornings in Keene were a weekly ritual for years and years. The widest Main Street in the world gave ample room for the crowds that gathered. (KPL)

ROYAL'S STORE in Colebrook was typical of village stores all over the state. What better place was there to swap the latest news, watch a parade, or just linger and chat! Pictured above, from left to right, are Ethan Titus, Ernest F. Royal, Guy B. Trask, Edd Atherton, and Guy Royal. The boy is Russell Simpson. Surrounded by all the good things to eat and drink are (*below,* left to right) Joe Jackson, Harry Alls, Casey Jones, Herbert Brigham, Carroll Jackson, and Ernest F. Royal. These 1906 scenes are gone for ever. The store was demolished in 1970 for—you guessed it—a parking lot. (Harry Alls)

THE NEW HAMPSHIRE LEGISLATURE IN 1905. Every Legislature in every session must have been photographed outside the State House. If the building looks tired, it is because it has held so many people throughout the years. Legislators are paid $200.00 a year, plus mileage, and some of them earn it. One ad-

vantage of its unwieldy size is that it makes corruption non-existent—unless you call it corruption to swap a vote for a ride home. (NHHS)

THE AMOSKEAG STEAMER (built in Manchester) makes an exhibition run down Main Street in Keene in 1906. Most New Hampshire fire departments are Volunteer or Call departments, staffed by clerks, mechanics, bank presidents, farmers, and barbers. And they're plenty fast. (KPL)

WINSTON CHURCHILL, New Hampshire's historical novelist ("The Crisis") ran as a reform candidate for Governor at the turn of the century. He lost, but the old convention system, dominated by Boston and Maine railroad interests, soon gave way to the direct primary. Churchill was Teddy Roosevelt's host in Cornish when the president visited there in 1902. (NHP)

PRESIDENT THEODORE ROOSEVELT addresses the veterans of the Grand Army of the Republic in Veterans Grove on August 28, 1902 which is today the site of the New Hampshire Veterans' Association headquarters at the Weirs. The President came to New Hampshire to mend some political fences, and to do a little fishing. (NHP)

TOWN FATHERS in New Hampshire still form the basic unit of government which continues today. Standing in this 1905 photo (left to right) are Colebrook's Jason Dudley (born without kneecaps), selectman and delegate to the Constitutional Convention, historian and fishing companion of Daniel Cummings, Town Clerk for 33 years, and Ed Hull, postman and selectman. There's little chance for corruption in small towns; there are too many people watching. (Harry Alls)

REPUBLICAN TICKET.

FOR PRESIDENT, | FOR VICE-PRESIDENT,

James A. Garfield. | Chester A. Arthur.

For Presidential Electors,

ARETAS BLOOD, of Manchester.
EZRA H. WINCHESTER, of Portsmouth.
ALBERT L. EASTMAN, of Hampstead.
JOHN A. SPALDING, of Nashua.
HENRY L. TILTON, of Littleton.

For Governor,

CHARLES H. BELL.

For Railroad Commissioners,

JAMES E. FRENCH,
CHARLES A. SMITH,
EDWARD J. TENNEY.

For Member of Congress,

EVARTS W. FARR.

ALBERT S. TWITCHELL, Councillor.
JOSEPH M. CLOUGH, Senator.

For County Officers,

MANSON S. BROWN..........................Sheriff.
ALVIN BURLEIGH ....Solicitor.
OSCAR C. HATCH.......................Treasurer.
JOHN E. HALL.......... ....Register of Deeds.
TYLER WESTGATE,..........Register of Probate.
WYMAN PATTEE, }
JOHN W. PEPPARD, } Commissioners.
ENOCH G. PARKER, }

THE REPUBLICAN TICKET usually won in New Hampshire. The Boston and Maine Railroad exerted great influence on state politics, partly through the lavish use of free railroad passes. (LML/PSC)

91

HAMPTON BEACH in the second decade of the century was well on its way to becoming a popular seaside resort. It was New Hampshire's answer to Coney Island. (NHP)

BIGNESS is just one word that describes the New Hampshire Great and General Court—the Legislature of the state. It is the third-largest legislative body in the English-speaking world, outranked only by the British Parliament and the U.S. House of Representatives. Within limits now imposed by the state constitution, membership fluctuates from session to session between 375 and 400 representatives. Prior to fixing the limit by referendum, the House had grown to 424 members. Reform attempts failed to cut the size of the House which all serious students of government describe as unwieldy, as most of the representatives are old House members jealously guarding its "democratic" make-up. Old Senator George Moses used to say that you could send a man off to the Legislature for the winter term with a clean collar and a $2.00 bill, and he'd come home in spring with the same collar and the same two-dollar bill. (NH/DRED)

THE BATTLESHIP *New Hampshire,* launched in 1908, and christened by the daughter of Governor John McLane. The ship had a length of 456′ 4″, a beam of 76′ 10″, and displaced 16,000 tons. The state of New Hampshire presented her with a magnificent Silver Service. She escorted troop ships to Europe during World War I and patrolled off Haiti during the Marine occupation. The battleship was decommissioned in 1921, and plans to build a successor were cancelled in 1943. (USN)

93

THE TREATY of the Russo-Japanese War focused the eyes of the world on the 56 men in this photograph—Russians and Japanese, as well as the Americans who arbitrated the conclusion of the Russo-Japanese War. The treat was signed in Portsmouth on September 5, 1905, a day of rejoicing for the civilized world. For Teddy Roosevelt, the achievement resulted in the Nobel Peace Prize, and for the historic port city, a place in the sun of public acclaim. (PPL)

ROBERT FROST in his Franconia study, 1915. No poet ever drew inspiration from his own soil more essentially than did Robert Frost in his New Hampshire years. He farmed in Derry, taught at Plymouth, and wrote exclusively in the accents he found from the White Mountains north. Lafayette was his favorite mountain, and today his home farm in Derry is being restored by concerned citizens of the state he loved most. (LML/PSC)

THE PAGEANT OF MERIDEN, this one in 1913, was an annual production presented by the prep-school boys of nearby Kimball Union in America's first bird sanctuary. (Kimball Union)

THE GUYOL GUARDS were organized when World War I came. The boys were too young to fight and the General was too old, so they formed their own army. General Joab N. Patterson drilled his three grandsons, the Guyol boys, and 13 of their friends into as fine a military outfit as ever paraded down the trolley tracks along North State Street on Memorial Day in Concord. The General had been wounded at Gettysburg, and later served as a Captain during the Spanish American War. (NHP)

"COW HAMPSHIRE" was the nickname given the New Hampshire College of Agriculture and Mechanic Arts after it moved to Durham in 1893, and for obvious reasons. It used to be said that on the farm they taught you where to throw it, and at Durham, they taught you how. The school became the University of New Hampshire in 1923, and was re-organized with three colleges—Liberal Arts, Technology, and Agriculture. These boys are judging a cow in a class in Dairy Husbandry. (UNH)

THE WORLD WAR MEMORIAL (*left*) in Exeter is the work of Daniel Chester French (shown below on a commemorative stamp) was the New Hampshire sculptor probably best-known for his statue of the seated Lincoln in the Lincoln Memorial in Washington. New Hampshire had 20,000 men in uniform in that war, and the lowest percentage of draft-dodgers in the nation, less than three percent. (NH/DRED-NHP)

THE AUXILIARY of the Son of Veterans of Seabrook poses in 1916 with the National Trophy banner proclaiming them to have the largest charter membership. The great days of lodge meetings would last another twenty-five years before the hub-bub of modern living and television would do much to curtail the social life provided by these organizations. (Peter Randall)

HARRY K. THAW, looking natty in a checked cap, is escorted to the Monadnock House in Colebrook following his capture by Sheriff Holman Drew. Thaw had recently escaped from a New York institution to which he had been committed for murdering Sanford White, whose attentions to Evelyn Nesbitt, the Girl in the Red Velvet Swing, made Thaw jealous. He was a lavish tipper, and this insured that a car was kept handy at all times in case he needed to return the eight miles to Canada. (Ruth Walker)

97

THE PORT OF ENTRY into Canada is just beyond the Indian Stream Republic and the Connecticut Lakes in Pittsburg. The lack of a road made it a tranquil station even in bootlegging days, and American Customs was housed in a trailer until the 1960s. Here, Conservation officer Harry Scott is checking the elevation.

FRENCH CANADIANS, along with Greeks, Russians, and Poles, have made a colorful addition to New Hampshire history. Some of the greatest woodsmen ever to swing an axe have come out of the state's North Country. The men in the picture are coming out of the woods near Clarksville; the man on the right is thought to be the first Therrien in New Hampshire. (NHF&G)

JIGGER JOHNSON, immortalized by Stewart Holbrook in "Holy Old Mackinaw," was the North Country's most famous living legend. In the words of his friend, Bob Monahan, he was "one of the toughest, hardest drinking, most courageous, kindliest and wisest man ever to come out of the timberlands." (Bob Monahan)

GEORGE VAN DYKE of Stewartstown, the greatest of the lumber barons, president of the legendary Connecticut Valley Lumber Company, came out of Canada as a barefoot kid, and by following his slogan "To hell with the man, save the cant dog," amassed a fortune. He ordered his driver to back up the car for a closer look at his drive at Turner Falls, and the car plunged down a bank, carrying him to his death. He was a tough man in a tough business. (Bob Shaw)

THE GREAT DAYS OF THE RIVER DRIVE, when labor was cheap and cant dogs cost money. Breaking up a log jam could be dangerous, but not as dangerous as fighting with a white-water man wearing caulked boots. The result of being stomped in the face by a pair of them was referred to as "lumberman's smallpox." (NHP)

A BATEAU was a slick way of easing about the river; larger craft were used as a cook shack and for transporting horses and men. The *Mary Ann* and the steamer *Diamond* were two such craft. (NHP)

MEAL TIME in a lumber camp was a time of silence. No talking was allowed; the men ate, and got out so that the "cookee" could clean up. Signs were posted to this effect; other signs warned the men not to spit on the floor. Food was plentiful, served cafeteria style, and waste was forbidden. (NHP)

THE SPRING PULPWOOD DRIVE on the Swift Diamond was a busy time; high water from the snow run-off insured good flotation. Rivers such as the Androscoggin would be wall-to-wall wood as the pulpwood floated on down to the Brown Company mills in Berlin. When the water level dropped, clean-up crews patrolled the banks and refloated any pulpwood left on the shore. (NHP)

THE GROVETON PAPER COMPANY was a North Country landmark, especially with its mountain of pulp wood awaiting conversion into paper. The Company sponsored a guessing contest at New Hampshire fairs, awarded prizes to whoever came closest to guessing the number of cords in a pile. The plant is a division of Diamond International today, and the home of Vanity Fair tissues. (NHP)

THE MACDOWELL COLONY (*left*) just outside the village of Peterborough, is a six hundred-acre artists' retreat founded in the early 1900s by the McDowell family. Here writers, composers, or painters could find either congeniality or solitude. Alec Waugh summed up what most other artists felt who came here: "All my life I have had the problem of finding a tranquil atmosphere in which to work and brood about my work . . . but I have never found any place as satisfactory as the McDowell colony." Edward A. McDowell (*above*), the founder, was an American composer. (NHP)

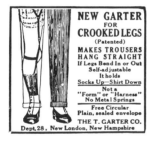

THE ENTERPRISE GARTER, invented by a Congregational minister, the Rev. John B. Koehne, was meant to hide men's bowed or knock-kneed legs. The advertisement appeared in the January 10, 1924 issue of *Life* magazine, offering this strange device that was hand-sewn by a few New London women of lavender sateen and elastic. It was sold by mail order only, since customers were bashful. (NHP)

THE SOCIETY for the Protection of New Hampshire Forests was campaigning in 1927 for $82,500.00 before March 1, 1928, to purchase the White Mountains area of 6,000 acres around the Old Man of The Mountains. The money was raised, and the area preserved, eventually becoming part of the National Forest system. (PNHF)

THE *New Hampshire Troubadour* was a beautiful little magazine that "sang the songs and praises of the Granite State." It was published monthly for 40,000 people, and was edited by Thomas Dreier, Donald Tuttle, and Andrew M. Heath. When the New Hampshire legislature, in its infinite wisdom, cut off its appropriation in 1951, it was a real loss to the state. (Doug Philbrick)

THE VERMONT BOUNDARY was typical of the complicated boundary disputes with all its neighbors which have marked New Hampshire's history. Royal orders eventually defined the Massachusetts (1741) and New York (1764) boundaries, while the state's northern boundary was set by the Webster-Ashburton Treaty (1842) which established the international line between the United States and Canada. But not until a 1934 U.S. Supreme Court ruling was the Vermont boundary decided. (NHP)

GOVERNOR JOHN WINANT was the youngest and one of the brightest governors in the nation at the time of his election in 1925. Named Ambassador to the Court of St. James by Franklin Roosevelt, Winant served with distinction throughout World War II. (NH/DRED)

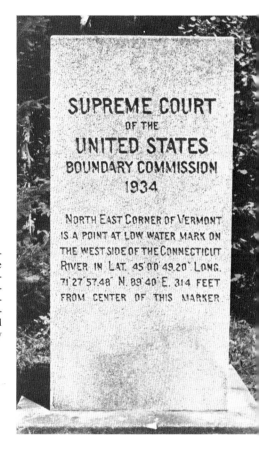

103

ROBB SAGANDORPH, founder of *Yankee* magazine in 1935, and publisher of *The Old Farmers Almanac* in Dublin, New Hampshire. (NHP)

THE HURRICANE OF 1938 caused more than 50 million dollars damage to New Hampshire forests. Winds exceeded 200 miles an hour on Mount Washington; this photo shows the white birch and fir damage in the Gale River Experimental forest in the White Mountain National Forest. (USFS)

MOUNT WASHINGTON in the fall as seen from Thorn Mountain in Jackson, New Hampshire. (NH/DRED)

THE CIVILIAN CONSERVATION CORPS found plenty to do in New Hampshire; they cut ski trails, fought forest fires, and built roads and fire towers. Perhaps their biggest contribution was in the North Country, where they strengthened the blood lines. The CCC was one of the most useful programs ever to come out of Washington. (USFS)

THE SNOW ROLLER was replaced by the plow, but who can forget the crunch of snow and the creak of the rollers? Telephone party lines carried news of its whereabouts, and sledding was great on the hard packed snow. This scene is in Dublin. (NHP)

ICE HARVESTING used to be big business after the January thaw. Unhappiness was falling in the frigid water, and staying up nights to keep the channel from freezing. But it was all worth it the following summer, when the ice man filled the ice box. (NHP)

BRINGING HOME the Christmas tree was always an easy job in New Hampshire, especially in the North Country where as many as 35 railroad cars full of trees would leave one town in the 1920s. Seen here are Mary and Peter Lund on the Gore Road in Lancaster. (NHP)

JANUARY THAW on the Connecticut River shows green water on the ice just south of Lancaster. (NH/DRED)

SAWING PULP with a buck saw was one way of keeping warm, and a sure way of raising ready cash. The man who cuts his own wood is twice warmed. (NHP)

THE ORDER OF EASTERN STAR was but one of many fraternal and paternal organizations that sponsored picnics, suppers, entertainments, and installations through the years. Though hurt by the advent of television and the faster pace of today's society, the Masons, the Odd Fellows, the Grange, and a dozen other organizations are still thriving today in New Hampshire. This O. E. S. group is from Colebrook and is holding its outing in the Whittermore opening in Dixville Notch in 1915. (Harry Alls)

THE AERIAL TRAMWAY seen here in 1934 in Franconia Notch makes the ascent up Cannon Mountain in eight minutes—an average skier will take twice that long to return. The tramway adds a touch of authenticity to a region known as "The Switzerland of America." (NH/DRED)

BAILEY'S STORE in West Springfield, about 1930. ". . . the lounging mirth of cracker barrel men, / snowed in by winter, spitting at the fire, / and telling the disreputable truth / with the sad eye that marks the perfect liar." Stephen Vincent Benet (NHP)

ARTHUR WALDEN, the famous sled driver, in front of a tent used in Admiral Byrd's Arctic Expedition, with six-year old Karluk, one of the dogs from the Woncelancet kennels which accompanied Byrd on his expedition. Walden was the first person to drive a dog team up Mount Washington to the summit and back (1929). (Peckett)

PECKETT'S OF SUGAR HILL was the forerunner of New Hampshire winter resorts to promote the joys of a vacation in the snow. This 1920s coasting scene was a hint of things to come, for in 1929 Pecketts established the first organized ski school in the United States by bringing Austria's Sig Buchmayr to this famous inn, where he pioneered in codifying what became known as The American Technique. (Peckett)

FLORENCE CLARK, the first and only woman to
drive a sled team to the summit of Mount Washington
and back. She could easily have lost her life several
times during the ordeal in April, 1932, when she was 32.
She is pictured here with Clarkso, her female lead dog,
who led a team of five dogs during the eight-hour climb
to the summit. Mrs. Clark also had the distinction of being the only woman to participate in a five-day race
from Berlin to Boston in the late 1920s. (Murray Clark)

A WINTER SCENE on Profile Lake. Nearby Laconia
often hosted the World Cup dog-sled races. (NH/
DRED)

THIS WINTER PANORAMA of Gunstock Mountain (left) and Belknap Mountain (right) is seen from Gunstock Lodge at Gilford, from where a ski tour and slalom trail led into the mountains. (NH/DRED)

EASTERN SLOPE
SKI SCHOOL

HANNES SCHNEIDER
AMERICAN BRANCH

CARROLL REED   •   Manager
BENNO RYBIZKA   •   Director
JACKSON AND NORTH CONWAY, N. H.

AMERICAN BRANCH of the Hannes Schneider Ski School, St. Anton am Arlberg, Tirol, Austria.

CAPABLE AMERICAN TEACHERS, trained by Benno Rybizka at the Hannes Schneider school in Austria.

CLASSES DAILY in Jackson and North Conway, December to April, for novice, intermediate and expert.

SPECIAL TRAINING in slalom and trail running for pupils of advanced classes.

MORE THAN 6000 lessons given by twelve instructors during the 1936-37 season to pupils of all grades of ability without a single accident.

ECCC ═══════════ ECCC

THE AIM of the Eastern Slope Ski School is to teach the principles of safety through control as it is taught at the famous Hannes Schneider Ski School in Austria, the oldest Alpine ski school, the principles of which have served as a basis for most of the other schools in the Alps.

THE ENTIRE STAFF of instructors, both in Jackson and North Conway, are under the supervision of Mr. Rybizka, thus assuring complete uniformity of instruction throughout all classes.

CLASSES ASSEMBLE DAILY in Jackson and North Conway at 10 A. M. and 2:30 P. M., when pupils are assigned to classes according to their ability. Classes are divided into many grades, permitting pupils to enter any day without previous arrangement. Punctuality is insisted upon.

THE SCHOOL TICKETS must be purchased in advance and are procurable at the Ski School headquarters in the Carroll Reed Ski Shops at Jackson and North Conway, or at your hotel.

TERMS:

  One day (2 classes) $2.00
  Week-end (Saturday and Sunday) 3.75
  Six days 10.00

Those unable to take a full day (two classes) may obtain at the Ski School offices a special half-day ticket for $1.25.

PRIVATE LESSONS may be arranged.

TICKETS MAY BE USED at any time during the season.

Address inquiries to
CARROLL REED
JACKSON, N. H.

CARROLL REED (at left in his North Conway Ski Shop) founded the Eastern Slope Ski School in December of 1936, America's first public ski school. It was a paradox that a man who had broken his back skiing and would never ski again did so much for skiing in New Hampshire; it was even more of a paradox that Hannes Schneider, former head ski instructor of the Austrian Army, came to North Conway from one of Hitler's concentration camps to liberate, as director of the Eastern Slope Ski School, thousands of ski students from the bondage of winter. (Carroll Reed)

FRESH POWDER at Cranmore Mountain, North Conway. (NH/DRED)

THE EARLY ROPE SKI TOW at Jackson. (NH/DRED)

HANNES SCHNEIDER teaching a class of instructors in front of the world's first skimobile, little cars that are easy to get in and out of with skis on. Schneider's release from Hitler's prison was arranged by Harvey Gibson, a former local boy who, as president of the Manufacturers Trust Company, was Germany's fiscal agent in this country at the time. Gibson purchased the old Randall Hotel and refurbished it as the Eastern Slope Inn. Eastern Slope Ski School sponsored the first qualified native ski instructors in North America by sending four local boys to Austria where they became professionals in the Arlberg technique. Carroll Reed stayed close to skiing by merchandising winter sports clothes and ski equipment in his Carroll Reed Ski Shops. (Carroll Reed)

THE SNOW TRAIN helped lure ski fans to North Conway. New England's first snow train left Boston for New Hampshire in 1931. The phenomenal "snow winter" of 1933-34 spawned thousands of recruits whose enthusiasm infected thousands in the following winters. These happy addicts, shown here singing "The Snow Train," boarded the special train at Boston before dawn. They came dressed for action, their luggage, skis, and poles. Hay-filled, horse-drawn pungs met them at the station and delivered them to the North Conway slopes. The trains were discontinued when the drunks outnumbered the skiers during the 1950s. (NHP)

THE BERLIN SKI JUMP (*facing page*) is the highest steel tower ski jump in the east, located at Berlin, New Hampshire. This 80-meter-high structure allows jumps as long as 350 feet. Instrumental in building this ski jump was Alf Halvorson (*right*) the coach of the 1932 Olympic Ski team of the United States. Halvorson also was an early president of Berlin's Nansen Ski Club, the oldest club of its type in America. He was elected in 1968 to the Ski Hall of Fame in recognition of his contribution to skiing not only in New England but in the entire country. (NH/DRED-Berlin Reporter)

IT'S A BUSY DAY at the ski shelter of the U.S. Forest Service at Tuckerman's Ravine, where skiing continues even into July. (NH/DRED)

DARTMOUTH COLLEGE SKATERS Viv Bruce ('40) and Paul Goodwin ('40) on their mark at the annual winter carnival. Dartmouth Winter carnivals began in 1910; the 1940 carnival, covered by Budd Schulberg and F. Scott Fitzgerald, emerged in Schulberg's book "What Makes Sammy Run," and on the late show as "Winter Carnival." (NH/DRED)

CARNIVAL NIGHT at Dartmouth was a highlight of carnival week; the Hanover campus featured huge ice-sculptures involving hundreds of man hours and tons of snow.

THE CONWAY CARNIVAL featured an iced bobsled run; steeper runs required more guts than brains. Winter sports were part and parcel of all such carnivals, this one in 1922. (USFS)

ON THE SHERBURNE TRAIL high on Mount Washington in the White Mountain National Forest. (NH/DRED-POTE)

A WINTER CAMP near Intervale in the late 1930s. Snowshoeing was still a popular sport, but giving way to cross-country skiing. Winter camping remains a sport for the hardy. (NH/DRED)

A LONE SKIER climbs Mount Washington; the view is to the south and towards Crawford Notch. (NH/DRED-POTE)

THE TOWN MEETING opened officially in Acworth with a blast of Sara Potter's horn. The town meeting is also the scene for the nation's first Presidential primary, held on the same day (to save money), the second Tuesday in March. Towns like Hart's Location, Millsfield, and Dixville Notch vie for the publicity of voting first-in-the-nation, a feat that can only be accomplished when 100% of the registered voters had voted so that the polls can be closed, usually at five seconds after midnight. (NHP)

THE VILLAGE SKATING RINK in Hill—a New Hampshire pastoral scene. (NH/DRED)

THE MEETING HOUSE at Newington, built in 1713, is the oldest meeting house in New Hampshire. De Tocqueville said that "Town Meetings are to liberty what primary schools are to science: they bring it within the people's reach; they teach men how to use and how to enjoy it." (NH/DRED)

WEATHER-WISE PEOPLE like Bryan Hicks and his mother Melinda could forecast spring by a dozen different signs. Mrs. Hicks slept in the same bed for 90 years; Bryan was a much sought-after water dowser who considered his talent for finding water with a forked stick "a divine gift." The old ways suit him best. (NHP)

RURAL FREE DELIVERY on the Dundee Road, North Conway to Jackson. Happiness is getting a new Spring catalog, "the Wish and Want Book." (NH/DRED-POTE)

THE TOWN BASKETBALL TEAM, the Mohawks from Colebrook, represented the best of an era in the early 1930s. Town teams existed all over the state, and town rivalries distinguished New Hampshire's unofficial indoor winter sport. The Mohawks were sponsored by a local ice cream company ("Taste Tells") and played basketball throughout New Hampshire, Maine, and Vermont for five years, highlighting their career in 1933 by defeating the Dartmouth varsity team. Pictured (left to right) are Oscar George Kelsea, Raymond Jordan, Lindsey Jordan, Richard Hughes, Henry Leavitt, and Carroll Colby. Seated is Wendall Newman. Missing from the picture is Kilburn "Pickles" Covell. (Dick Hughes)

STATE CHAMPION for two years running was North Stratford High School's six-man team. Coached by Don Harriman, considered the best coach in the entire state, North Stratford's small squad was drawn from a school which registered just 40 boys. Their opponents always claimed Stratford players were issued basketballs before books; the picture shows the team that defeated Charlestown (42-28) for their second State title. Seated, (left to right) are Dennis Hovey, Alphonse Bergeron, Chet Roby, Errol Richardson, Bert LaPointe. Rear, Milton Paradis, Coach Don Harriman. (NSHS)

123

THE PEABODY RIVER looking upstream toward Pinkham Notch with surface water eating away at the March snow. (NH/DRED-POTE)

GATHERING SAP with the aid of a 100-year-old sap yoke and wooden buckets is passe today in an age of plastic pipe, but Manson Smith's Sugar Grove in East Hebron also featured oxen back in 1938. (NH/DRED)

A SUGARING-OFF PARTY near Columbia in 1920 featured hand-whittled paddles and buckets of snow at the ready. (Harry Alls)

TYING HOOKS to a fish line is a common sight aboard any fishing boat; New Hampshire's 18-mile coast line is the shortest of any state in the nation, and its waters in constant dispute between Maine and New Hampshire lobstermen. (NHP)

OLD BLACKSMITH SHOP in Lancaster owned by Robert Addley is a scene fast disappearing from the face of New Hampshire. (NH/DRED-SHOREY)

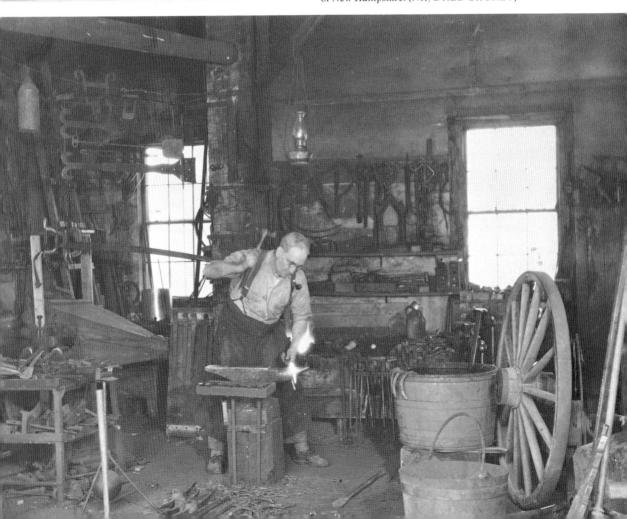

A WHITE HORSE was worth 25 points in roadside cribbage, a game played by children riding in a car; M. E. Blaisdell of Goffstown is shoeing this one. (NHP)

SPRING HARROWING with a 6-horse power harrow near Gorham, with Mount Madison and Mount Adams in the background. (NH/DRED-POTE)

STOCKING A POND with fish is a happy sight anytime; the New Hampshire Fish and Game Department's tank truck cut fish mortality drastically. Conservation officers also have a full-time job every fall rounding up lost deer hunters from Massachusetts. (NH/DRED)

BOAT LAUNCHING with the Isles of Shoals in the background. (NH/DRED)

Oh Earth! thy summer song of joy may soar
Ringing to heaven in triumph. I but crave
the sad, caressing murmur of the wave
that breaks in tender music on the shore.   from "Landlocked" by Celia Thaxter

COVERED BRIDGE over Perry Stream in Pittsburg. (NH/DRED)

COVERED BRIDGE interior in Bradford. Carved initials, many within hearts, decorated the interior of most bridges, before the interiors were lighted. Covered bridges protected lovers as well as the floors. (NH/DRED-Manahan)

> *"Here was a refuge from the sudden showers*
> *that swept like moving music field and wood,*
> *and here, cool tunneled dark, when sultry hours*
> *danced with white feet beyond the bridge's hood,*
> *yet there are souless men whose hand and brain*
> *tear down what time will never give again."*
>
> Andrew M. Scruggs

TARIFF OF TOLL RATES varied with the traffic. Common to many was the admonition "Walk or Pay Two Dollars." The warning referred to the vibrations caused by trotting horses that could weaken the bridge. (NHP)

TARIFF OF TOLL RATES

EACH FOOT PASSENGER	
BICYCLES, EACH RIDER	2¢
HORSE AND RIDER	2¢
HORSE, JACK, MULE, NEAT BEAST, SHEEP OR SWINE, EACH	5¢
ANY VEHICLE DRAWN BY ONE HORSE OR BEAST	2¢
ANY VEHICLE DRAWN BY TWO HORSES OR BEASTS	10¢
ANY VEHICLE DRAWN BY THREE HORSES OR BEASTS	15¢
ANY VEHICLE DRAWN BY FOUR HORSES OR BEASTS	20¢
ANY VEHICLE DRAWN BY MORE THAN FOUR HORSES OR BEASTS, FOR EACH ADDITIONAL HORSE OR BEAST	25¢
	5¢
AUTOMOBILES, PASSENGER (SEVEN PASSENGERS OR LESS)	15¢
AUTOMOBILES, PASSENGER (MORE THAN SEVEN PASSENGERS)	25¢
AUTOMOBILE TRUCKS, LESS THAN 1 TON	15¢
AUTOMOBILE TRUCKS, 1 TON OR MORE	25¢
MOTORCYCLES, ONE PASSENGER	
MOTORCYCLES, WITH SIDE CAR, (TWO PASSENGERS)	

SHARPENING A SCYTHE has nearly become a lost art. (NHP)

RAKING HAY at the foot of Sandwich Notch; what is hotter than love and haying? (NH/DRED-DORIS DAY)

MILKING COWS BY HAND went out with the advent of milking machines. Hundreds of small New Hampshire family farms have vanished within the last thirty years, and with them a way of life. (NHP)

130

SALT HAY in the Hampton marshes is still used around tomato plants because it's free from weeds. (NHP)

HAY TIME in Jefferson with lady tourists lending a helping hand. Mount Starr King (named for the novelist) is in the background. When you met a load of hay, you were supposed to make a wish. (NH/DRED-POTE)

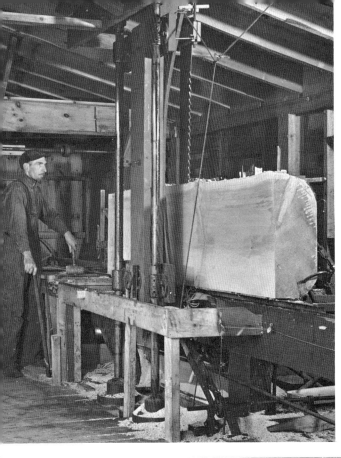

ONE OF THE LAST "Up-and-Down" saws in New Hampshire at Goffe's Mill in Bedford. Water power was the key to New Hampshire's mills; you don't see many logs that size any more! (NH/DRED-EAMES)

LAKE WINNIPEASAUKEE in the summer with the *Mount Washington* steaming in the background. The nearby Weirs was named for the funnel-shaped fish traps set by the Indians. (NHP)

THIS MOUNTAIN CLIMBER in Franconia Notch must have been practicing for the climb behind him. The sport has claimed a dozen lives through the years in this region. (NH/DRED-JOHN WILSON)

WHITE WATER canoeing through the rapids below Littleton. (NH/DRED)

A CAMP ON BIG DIAMOND POND involved the 99-year lease of a 50-by-700-foot lot at $10.00 a year from the Town of Stewartstown in 1903. The fish never bit as good as the black flies, and the neighborhood deteriorated; but a camp is a camp in New Hampshire, and never a cottage. (Harry Alls)

CAMP OSSIPEE was typical of New Hampshire summer camps for boys and girls; there were 218 camps in the state by 1950, housing 23,000 young people and 3,000 counselors. Camp Chocorua, the first boy's camp, was organized on Squam Lake in 1881, and the first girl's camp on New Found Lake in 1900. New Hampshire was the birthplace of the organized camp movement. (NH/DRED)

CAMP ARCADIA at the Weirs in 1948. Counselors taught a love of the countryside, constructive habits, a knowledge of aquatics and sports, and ethical spiritual values. (NH/DRED)

FISHING on the Connecticut River near North Stratford, with the Percy Peaks in the background. The Connecticut River rises in Pittsburg's Connecticut lakes, and contains some of the best fishing of its kind in the world. (NH/DRED-POTE)

PHILLIPS EXETER ACADEMY is the state's oldest Boy's Preparatory school. Founded in 1788, its graduates have included the sons of four American presidents, including Abraham Lincoln's son Robert. The Revolutionary capital of the New Hampshire Province, Exeter is considered by many to be the state's most beautiful town. (NH/DRED-ORNE)

ST. PAUL'S IN CONCORD has always been considered one of the finest preparatory schools in the nation; it is renown for academic excellence. (NHP)

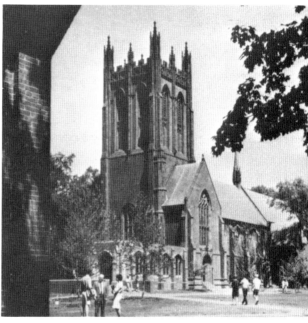

JUNE WEEK at Kimball Union proves that some things are changeless. (KU-Spaulding)

Still rises o'er Chocorua's grave
the mighty tombstone with his name
and still the quiet waters lave
the shore where crimson sunsets flame.

Marion Logan

(NH-DRED)

137

THE GLEN ELLIS FALLS in Pinkham Notch are one of the most photographed scenic sites in the state; this photograph was taken by the U.S. Forestry Service, and marked with the notation, "Do not send out." (USFS)

LOBSTER MAN Ben Saunders of Rye Harbor posed with one of New Hampshire's most famous natural resources. Constant bickering with Maine over the exact boundary at sea has marked the lobster industry in more recent years. Lobster tastes best when cooked in sea water. (NH/DRED-ORNE)

THE NEW HAMPSHIRE SEACOAST is only 18 miles long, the shortest in the nation. University of New Hampshire students are reminded in their Alma Mater that "Behind thee tow'r the mountains, before thee roars the sea." With the beach just minutes away, it was always a temptation to cut classes and roar beside the sea. (NH/DRED-HAND)

YANKEE INDEPENDENCE is preserved in New Hampshire by such people as seventy-year old Fred Manchester, when he ran into trouble with the Lebanon police for parking his horse and buggy in the Common. He tied up in front of the Police Station and won a permanently reserved parking place. (NHP)

THIS ROAD SIGN was the result of the people living up ahead being asked just once too often, "Is this Columbus Jordan Road?" (NHP)

139

A SPITE FENCE near Ossipee, built by Thomas Plant, a self-made millionaire and an admirer of Napoleon Bonaparte. When he was turned down trying to buy his neighbor's land, he built this fence of cast-off lumber and other junk directly across the street in their full view. Nothing prevailed; he was unable to buy the land until after the neighbor's death. (NHP-ROBIE)

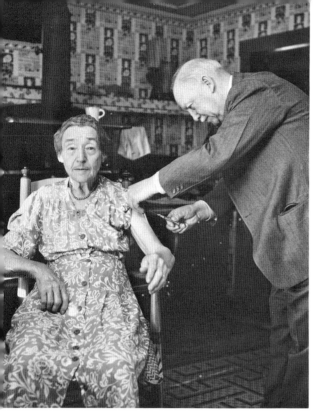

HOUSE CALLS are getting to be something in the past; here Mabel Mitchell of Nottingham gets a shot from Dr. Fred Fernald, a friend since grammar school days. The doctor's practice covers a 600-square-mile area. Many physicians of northern New Hampshire practice in three states and Canada. (NH/DRED-ARMSDEN)

AUCTION TIME is a social event anywhere in the state as here in Dublin. No one who claims to have New Hampshire in his blood could possibly hold something called a "garage sale" and keep his self-respect. (NH/DRED-ORNE)

AGGIE SWEATT of Errol had been on the job for forty years when this picture was taken, ever since Errol got its first telephone and pay station in 1921. Direct dialing took something out of New Hampshire life, something irretrievably lost. (NHP/WHITNEY)

A CHECKER GAME being filmed in Tamworth. Pasteurized milk took a lot of getting used to when it first came in; there was no cream on top of the bottle, it wouldn't sour, and it tasted funny. If you know a farmer, its still possible to get raw milk. (NH/DRED)

"THE OLD HOMESTEAD" is New Hampshire's passion play, first performed in Swanzey during haying time in 1886. It toured the country for over ten years and played every major city from New York to San Francisco. Revived in 1941 to pay off the church mortgage in Swanzey Center, it is performed nightly for three nights in July at the full of the moon by members of the Congregational Church and members of the North Swanzey Community Association. The play employs 250 people, and recreates a nostalgic bit of New Hampshire's past. (NH/DRED-SANFORD)

THE *Boston Post* CANE was a gold-headed cane of gaboon ebony from the Congo, presented to the oldest man in every New Hampshire town by the *Boston Post* in 1909, and handed down. The Pittsburg cane was presented to Henry Scott Lord on Old Home Day, when he was 84. He held it for 9 years until his death at 93. Shown seated next to him in 1944 is his son Will, Will's son William, and William's son Stephen. (Bill Lord)

142

BEAN-HOLE BEANS at the Chichester Old Home Day in 1942 are proudly displayed by Samuel C. Marden, who cooked them. (NH/DRED)

BEDFORD'S PRESBYTERIAN CHURCH is a real beauty, but the Congregational Church is New Hampshire's unofficial state church; Sunday service is at eleven o'clock, and funerals are at two o'clock. (NH/DRED-SANFORD)

THE VILLAGE OF WHITEFIELD is typical of small New Hampshire towns where Old Home Day has been celebrated since 1899 when Gov. Frank Rollins first established it. Whitefield was the home of America's oldest summer theatre, the Chase Barn Playhouse, before it burned in the 1960s.

*"Come and join us in New Hampshire,
    for her valleys now are green;
and her hilltops in the distance
    make an old familiar scene.
Glad the hands that are extended,
    while all nature, flower gay,
has a smiling welcome ready
    for all comers Old Home Day."*

OLD HOME DAY is a time for catching up, as these ladies are doing at a tea during the Sandwich Old Home Day in 1942. (NH-DRED)

THE GREEK PEOPLE in Manchester are served by Fr. Stephen Papadoulias at St. George's Hellenic Community Church, focal point of the largest Greek community in New Hampshire. Greeks left the poverty of their homeland from 1905 on, and immigrated to American textile and shoe factories anxious for their cheap labor. (NHP-Sanford)

SAWING WOOD wasn't every boy's idea of summer fun in 1943, but family farms required a lot of work from every member, and with a war on, pulp was in big demand. These young brothers are working in Coos county. (NH/DRED)

THE PITTSBURG GUIDE SHOW is a North Country institution held in connection with Old Home Day. This 1960 photo shows some of the action that has been going on for years. The New Hampshire Guide's Association is one of the most colorful groups in the state. Pittsburg women have always been just as good as the men, whether at canoe racing or dropping a deer. (NH/DRED-CARROLL)

YOUTH IS KITTENISH, and old age is sewing a chair mat at the age of 87. Longevity must be in the mountain air in New Hampshire. (NH/DRED)

ARTS AND CRAFTS feature native ingenuity; dried weeds and cones are fashioned into attractive decorations by Thressa Nelson. Cold winter nights produce patchwork quilts and hooked rugs of intricate design, and what is warmer than hand-knitted socks and mittens? (NH/DRED)

AN EAGER HORSE on his way to thrill the exhibitors and competitors in the pulling contest at the Hopkinton Fair. A man can't be too careful when he connects a raring-to-go horse to a load of stones. (NH/DRED-Whitney)

147

NATURE'S BOUNTY is a prize-winning attraction at the Pittsfield Fair; New Hampshire fairs have flourished for a hundred years, and exhibits such as this one reflect a pride in agriculture that remains undiminished in New Hampshire. (NH/DRED-SANFORD)

A TUG OF WAR through a turned-on hose at the Lancaster Fair is a sidelight of New Hampshire's largest agricultural fair sponsored for more than 70 years by the Coos and Essex Agricultural Society. (NH/DRED)

148

THE HILLBILLY BAND was an institution for three decades in the North Country; the band made the transition from square dancing through the Latin American craze, Rock and Roll, to old fashioned cheek-to-cheek dancing with no apparent change of tempo. Shown here at one of the hundreds of Saturday night dances at Pittsburg's Tall Timber Lodge are (left to right) Vernon Hawes, Del Fish, Claudice Young at the piano, and Willie Hawes. Claire Young is partically obscured by Bryan Avery, a recent captain of the steamboat *Mount Washington.* (VERNON HAWES)

WHITE TAILED DEER were always a New Hampshire attraction, whether running wild or pleasing the tourists. Frank Baldwin's deer were a famous stop in Pittsburg en route to the Connecticut Lakes.

JACK-O-LANTERN time meant wood for the winter and pleasing a small boy with an artful knife. Nobody seems to whittle anymore. (NH/DRED-Armsden)

*"Before green apples blush,
  before green nuts embrown
why, one day in the country
  is worth a month in town."*
Christina Rossetti (NH/DRED)

FIRST CONNECTICUT LAKE near the top of New Hampshire is one of four lakes that feed the mighty Connecticut river, New Hampshire's natural boundary with Vermont. One of the last wilderness areas in the state, and long famous for its fishing and hunting, this north country region is New Hampshire's port of entry into Canada. Just south of here is the only place in the state where you can step across the Connecticut River, and remain in New Hampshire. (NH/DRED-Bicknell)

THE *USS Squalus,* commissioned on March 1, 1939, in Portsmouth where it was built, was still on its sea trials when it made a test dive on May 23rd. An unclosed valve caused the submarine to plunge to a depth of forty fathoms between the New Hampshire coast and the Isles of Shoals. Twenty-six men perished, and thirty-three were rescued by means of a diving bell. After many unsuccessful attempts, the boat was raised later that year and completely rebuilt and recommissioned as the *USS Sailfish.* She went on to establish a brilliant record in the Pacific during World War II, climaxed by the sinking of the Japanese carrier *Chuyo* on December 4, 1945, for which she received the Presidential Unit Citation. This remarkable picture by the *Boston Post* shows her breaking to the surface when she was finally raised. (BOSTON POST)

NEW HAMPSHIRE PULLETS on Governor Dale's desk in 1947 were raised by Andrew Christie (right) of Kingston. Chicken pie suppers were a great way to raise money for the church or the Grange. (NH/DRED)

A MOUNTAIN OF DISHES from a chicken pie supper, or an Old Home Day supper such as this scene in Middleton is the lot of women throughout the state. Male organizations tend more towards Oyster Stew—with fewer dishes. (NH-DRED-Stephen Whitney)

Preceding page: MOUNT WASHINGTON and the Ammonoosuc River—a majestic but peaceful panorama. (NH/DRED)

BETTE DAVIS came to Littleton in 1941 to celebrate her birthday (*left*) and to attend the world premiere of her latest picture, "The Great Lie." Escorted to the theatre (*below*) by Gov. Robert O. Blood (right) and U.S. Senator Styles Bridges (left), she drew the largest crowd in Littleton's history. Bette Davis lived several summers at "Butternut Lodge," her home in nearby Sugar Hill. (Littleton CofC)

DARTMOUTH NAVY ROTC unit parades in dress uniform at graduation ceremonies in early days of World War II. The Morrill Act of 1862 established the legal basis for "land grant" colleges; all New Hampshire land grant colleges supported the Naval or Army Reserve Officer's Training Corps. (NH/DRED)

LOUIS De ROCHEMONT of Newington (pointing left) was on location at the New Hampshire seacoast in the early 1940s when making the movie "We Are the Marines." The academy-award-winning producer had made such New Hampshire-related movies as "New England's Eight Million Yankees," "Whistle at Eaton Falls," and "Lost Boundaries." In 1935, Louis de Rochemont began to produce "The March of Time," which ultimately attracted an audience of 40 million people world-wide. This innovative monthly series introduced pictorial journalism to movie-making, and assured de Rochement a place in the annals of American cinematrography. (George Black)

GERMAN POW'S brought World War II home to New Hampshire when 250 of Rommel's Afrika Korps were imprisoned in Stark where they cut wood for the Brown Company at eighty cents a day. Several escaped; all but one were recaptured, who was discovered living in New York City years later, married and raising a family. No charges were preferred.

POTATO PICKING in Newfields during World War II meant half-sessions of school and extra pocket money at 7¢ a bushel. New Hampshire school children purchased 5 million dollars of War Bonds and Stamps; younger children collected 12,000 bags of milkweed floss for life jackets, plus uncounted tons of scrap paper. (NH/DRED-ORNE)

156

WILLIAM LOEB (*above*) purchased New Hampshire's only state-wide paper *The Manchester Union Leader* on November 1, 1946, and promptly became—and remains—the most controversial man in the state. He published a statement of his intentions (*left*) on this occasion. (*Laconia Citzen*)

THE GREAT DROUGHT AND FIRES OF 1947. Hundreds of acres of New Hampshire woodlands and thirty towns were threatened during the great drought that afflicted all New England in 1947. On October 15, following a 26-day drought, the woods were closed, but fires broke out in Laconia, Raymond, Portsmouth, and Rye. High winds swept in fire from Maine, three houses burned near Province Lake; Bald Mountain near Sunappee burned, a great blaze raged in Hampstead and Atkinson. Families were evacuated near Framington, and the Sandwich fire threatened the White Mountain National Forest. Students from Dartmouth, UNH, and Plymouth Teacher's College were organized into fire-fighting units. Finally, Federal agencies united "Operation Cirrus," and two B-17's seeded the cloud banks at 18,000 feet. A light rain followed, and the fires ended. (NH/DRED)

RENE GAGNON, Private First Class, USMC, points to himself in famed Rosenthal photo of flag raising on Iwo Jima's Mount Suribachi. The photo was used in 7th War Bond Drive poster; Gagnon posed for his own likeness in Washington's Marine Memorial where, as one of two survivors, he spoke at its dedication. (USMC)

THE CATHEDRAL OF THE PINES in Ringe (*below*) was dedicated to the Glory of God in loving memory of Lt. Sanderson Sloane (*right*) as a place where all people may come and worship, each in his own way. The cross is of New Hampshire granite, and the Altar of Nations contains stones from every state in the Union, from Presidents of the United States and from world dignitaries. The hurricane of 1938 helped create the "cathedral;" Lieutenant Sloane, who was shot down over Germany during World War II, would have built his postwar home on the site. (NH/DRED)

JAMES F. O'NEIL on parade in Manchester on Homecoming Day October 18, 1947 following his election as National Commander of the American Legion. Former Manchester Police Chief is accompanied by Maurice F. Devine, who nominated him for the office. "Jimmie" went on to become publisher of AMERICAN LEGION MAGAZINE. (James F. O'Neil)

THE WATCHER (or, as it is sometimes called, the Old Woman of the Mountain), New Hampshire's most haunting face, gazes down on Franconia Notch as it has since the state was born. (NH/DRED)

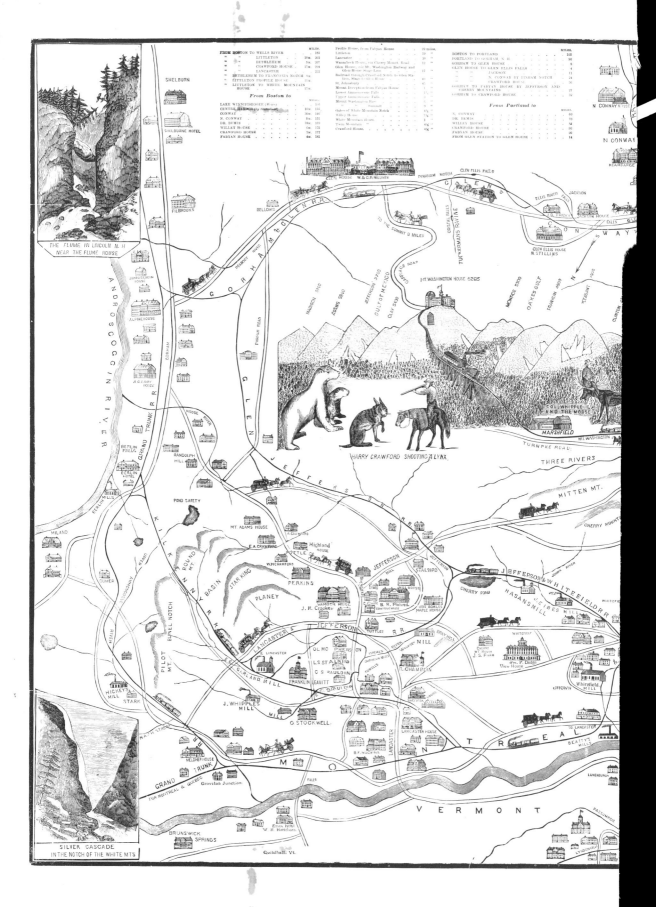